∽ Critical Acclaim for ∾

Ending Elder Abuse: A Family Guide

"…an invaluable contribution to a significant part of our nation's population—the elderly. Sandell and Hudson…touch the lives of the elderly and their families all over the nation."
— *Christopher Cox, Former US Congressman, Newport Beach, California*

"I thank Diane Sandell for her years of hard work and devotion to the cause of bringing the many aspects of elder abuse into public focus. This book will help all of us to better understand the problem."
— *John R. Lewis, Former Senator, 33rd District, Orange, California*

"Sandell's story makes an important statement about a national disgrace. It serves as a blueprint for evaluating eldercare facilities."
— *Joel Wachs, Former Councilman, 2nd District, City of Los Angeles*

"This beautiful book is a family love story, filled with practical suggestions and information on caring for an aging loved one. A must-read for adult children of aging parents."
— *Pamala D. McGovern, Former Executive Director Council on Aging, Orange County, Santa Ana, California*

"An important and timely book that opens our eyes to the horror of elder abuse; offers constructive, positive step-by-step plans of actions for families, the long-term care facilities and the medical profession."
— *Mary Allen, Former President, Board of Directors, Orange County (CA) Council of Aging, Ombudsman Program, Irvine, California*

"(Sandell's) individual efforts have made a difference in many lives over a considerable period of time… I can enthusiastically endorse (this book) as a much needed document."
— *Ruth Cambron, Ombudsman Program Consultant, California Department of Aging, Sacramento, California*

"This book held my undivided attention. I did no scanning. Just reading. Hanging onto every word. Wishing they were not true. Knowing they were. And my advice to any family seeking to place a loved one in a nursing home is: read *Ending Elder Abuse*."
— *Mary Jane Holt, The Citizen, Fayetteville, Georgia*

"Having friends who struggle as members of the sandwich generation, that large percentage of the population dealing with both adult children living at home and elderly parents, I highly recommend this book. Particularly useful are the suggestions on how to handle the frustrations: just to know, "Wow, I'm not the only one who feels that way"—gives hope and comfort in an otherwise seemingly hopeless situation. This is a must-read for anyone whose parent is losing his or her independence. Whom to talk to? What to do? Where to go for help? When to act? How to deal with the emotions? These and many more questions are answered and issues addressed."
— *Pamela Caldwell, Senior Editor,* Precious Times Magazine

"When I finished reading this touching book, I felt as though I had been in the presence of the Holy! I had approached it as simply an informative book that would help me assure the safety of my mentally handicapped and visually challenged brother-in-law, who resides in an assisted living facility. What a wonderful surprise it was to discover the spiritual nature of this invaluable resource. I highly recommend *Ending Elder Abuse* to all caregivers of aging relatives who are seeking a practical guide that provides an encounter with the Holy as a bonus!"
— *Pastor Jimmie H. Melton, Cornerstone Presbyterian Church, Concord, N.C.*

"For any of us contemplating nursing home care for a parent, or already have a parent in a care situation outside the home, Ending Elder Abuse offers what we most need and want: clarity about the issues; practical guidance for the caregiver; truth about the frequency of substandard care of the elderly; vignettes that enable each of us to face the realities of eldercare with honesty and integrity; questions that must be asked; resource information; and throughout, a great compassionate care for the elders we love. Sandell and Hudson have given us a gift that will help us negotiate the long, complex, and often dangerous journey."
— *Maria Sirois, Psy.D., author of*
Every Day Counts: Lessons in Love, Faith and Resilience

"Valiant, noble, and eloquent efforts on behalf of senior citizens and residents of long-term care facilities."
— *Marc B. Hankin, Attorney at Law, Los Angeles, California*

"A positive approach to informing the public of the issues and their rights, and offering practical help for everyone who seeks to deal with the provider and patient care-giver issues relating to our own aging bodies as well as of those we love."
— *Dr. John Crandall, Portola Hills, California*

CRITICAL ACCLAIM

"This book will be of tremendous value to the millions of families faced with the dilemma of having to place their elderly loved ones in long-term care facilities, and to those whose loved ones have suffered abuse in them."
— *Chris J. Van Ruiten, President, Leisure Consultants, Inc.*

"A valuable book that belongs in every household library. Filled with well-founded advice and sound proposals for improving the lives of the aged, whether they are cared for in their own homes, in their children's homes, or in long-term care facilities."
— SilverLinings

"THE BOOK to read about caregiving for our elderly loved ones. It will no doubt be welcomed by all who provide services to the elderly, but it will have even greater value for those who have yet to realize the challenges that lie ahead."
— *Donna J. Vohar, Attorney at Law, Conway, Pennsylvania*

"Your book will be an inspiration as well as an educational guide for dealing with this unpleasant subject in a positive manner. Thank you for giving me the opportunity to share in this endeavor by offering my wholehearted endorsement."
— *Randa R. Mendenhall, licensed tourist guide, Washington, D.C.*

"Your story will touch many hearts, and move people to take a stand and make the changes that we as a society need to make. You are a beacon of hope."
— *Linda Scheck, former executive director*
Alzheimer's Association of Orange County, Calif.

"This book will change the lives of those who read it."
— *Sandra Ann Hagan, President, Board of Directors, NOBLE*
(Network Outreach—Better Living for the Elderly), Knoxville, Tennessee

"An important story. Diane Sandell's courage is an inspiration, and her efforts to find solutions show us what needs to be done."
— *Kent Shocknek, CBS2 News, Los Angeles, California*

"An invaluable resource for everyone faced with caring for a loved one. The authors take the helplessness and fear out of a difficult task and lead us through it sanely and compassionately. I suggest this book to everyone. In fact, it should be in every doctor's office in the nation."
— *Barbara Johnson Witcher,*
author of Create the Job You Love and Make Plenty of Money

Ending
Elder Abuse

◡ a family guide ◡
Revised Edition

Diane S. Sandell & Lois Hudson

how you can
protect your loved ones ◆ evaluate facilities
partner with the medical community ◆ take care of yourself
motivate legislators and government officials
and what to do if things go wrong

QED
Press
FORT BRAGG
CALIFORNIA

Published by QED Press
155 Cypress Street
Fort Bragg, California 95437
(707) 964-9520
Fax: (707) 964-7531
http://www.cypresshouse.com

Book production by Cypress House
Cover and book design by Michael Brechner
Cover photograph Copyright © 2008 David Sucsy, iStock Images,
All Rights Reserved

Library of Congress Cataloging-in Publication Data

Sandell, Diane S., 1937-
    Ending elder abuse : a family guide / Diane S. Sandell and Lois Hudson.
      p. cm.
    Reprint. Originally published in 2000.
    Includes index.
    ISBN 978-0-936609-43-0 (pbk. : alk. paper)
    1. Older people--Abuse of--United States. 2. Aging parents--Abuse of--United States. 3. Nursing home patients--Abuse of--United States. 4. Aging parents--Care--United States. 5. Aging parents--Family relationships--United States. 6. Adult children of aging parents--Family relationships--United States. 7. Adult children of aging parents--United States--Attitudes. I. Hudson, Lois, 1933- II. Title.
    HV6626.3.S26 2010
    362.6--dc22   2009018966

Printed in the USA
2 4 6 8 9 7 5 3 1
Revised Edition

Dedicated to

∽ Bessie and Virgie ∾

Two of a Kind

Disclaimer

This book was created to provide information on safeguarding elders from abuse. It is sold with the understanding that the publisher and authors are not engaged in rendering legal or other professional services. If legal or other expert assistance is required, the advice of competent professionals should be sought.

It is not the purpose of this book to reprint all the material that is otherwise available to those in need of information on the subject of elder abuse prevention. The information herein is derived from the authors' personal experience, and is intended to complement, supplement, and amplify the existing body of literature pertaining to elder abuse. You are urged to read all the available material, learn as much as possible about the subject, and tailor the information to your individual needs. For more information, please explore the many resources available in your local library and on the Internet.

There is no quick, simple formula for preventing elder abuse. Those who wish to become involved in this complex and sometimes-frustrating subject must expect to invest considerable time and energy in order to derive the maximum benefit, both for caregivers and the elders so needful of their caring.

Every effort has been made to make this book as complete and as accurate as possible. However, *there may be mistakes*, both typographical and in content. Therefore, this text should be used only as a general guide, and not as the ultimate source of information about elder abuse. Furthermore, this book may contain information that is current only up to the printing date.

The purpose of this book is to educate, comfort, and inspire. The authors and QED Press shall have neither liability nor responsibility to any person or entity with respect to any loss or damage caused, or alleged to have been caused, directly or indirectly, by the information contained in this book.

If you do not wish to be bound by the above, you may return this book to the publisher for a full refund.

Contents

ACKNOWLEDGMENTS

We, the authors, wish to express our appreciation to our families:
  To my husband, Jim, who stands alone, my gift, who was, and
  is, always there through better or worse, forever, my love; to my
  sister, Betty Lane, who has walked the years with me, with deep
  appreciation and respect, my love.

To my children , who always stand by me:
  Kathy Lane and Jim, Mark and Dorie, Kimberly and Jon, always,
  my love; to my grandchildren, Brittney, Rebecca, Patrick, Kevin,
  and James.

$XXXOOO$, 5/3.

DSS

To my family:
  Roger, in remembrance; Jim and Kathy and Patrick; Bob and Heidi,
  thank you, with love.

LH

To the following, for their encouragement, support, and assistance:
  Carole Herman, Foundation Aiding the Elderly, mentor and colleague;
  Pamala D. McGovern and *Rochelle Woolery,* Orange County Council
  on Aging—Ombudsman; *Ivan R. Nichols, M.D.; Donald R. Gilchrist,*
  Wendy J. Lee, and *Ann Abajian,* for assistance in legislative areas;
  Linda Scheck, Orange County Chapter Alzheimer's Association;
  Ruth Cambron, California Ombudsman Program Consultant;
  Julie Schoen, California Health Insurance Counseling Advocacy
  Program; *Keith D. Wisbaum,* Attorney at Law, specializing in Elder
  Abuse litigation; *Ann Simons,* for her beautiful poem; *Dirk DeWolfe,*
  Executive Administrator, Town and Country Manor; and to the
  many others, without whom none of this would have been possible,
  Thank you.

To the following at QED Press for their faith and patient assistance in making an impossible dream come true:

Cynthia Frank, Joe Shaw, Mike Brechner, and Hannah Cochran.

To those who have graciously endorsed our work.

The publisher wishes to thank these individuals and businesses for their generous help with this book:

Michael E. Brown, M.D.; John T. Wallace, M.D.; and *Charles Bush*, Executive Director of the Fort Bragg Senior Center, for their invaluable comments on the manuscript; *Michele Rubin* and *Alia Levine*, of Writers House, for their encouragement; *Sal Glynn*, for his publishing expertise and wise counsel; *Gopa Design and Illustration*, for characteristic grace under pressure, and the *staff of QED Press*, for their dedication and perseverance.

FOREWORD

Ending Elder Abuse is a vital tool to increase the odds of obtaining a satisfactory long-term care facility experience for your elderly relatives who can no longer live on their own. Few seniors choose to move out of their home and into a care facility. Well-intentioned family members typically make this decision knowing little more than general information about the facility's location, services, and amenities.

While health and safety needs are certainly high priorities, a sensitive and essential focus also requires a keen awareness that your loved one will be entirely dependent on staff to administer quality care for all activities of daily living faithfully, thoughtfully, and in a timely manner. Diane Sandell and Lois Hudson provide just such a perspective.

Promotional literature with photos of attentive staff and smiling residents presents a scenic and serene portrait of a smooth-running facility, but newspaper accounts of facilities charged with serious health and safety violations tell a different story. *Ending Elder Abuse* helps you go far beyond the fancy brochures so that your loved one is much more likely to receive quality care as a direct result of your family becoming involved, in a positive manner, with the long-term care facility's system for managing daily care-giving services.

For seniors and their families, the nursing-home fear might be that no one is watching or no one cares, but as the authors point out, it doesn't have to be that way. This thought-provoking book will teach you many effective ways to help your loved one receive the necessary care and treatment — resulting in our elders enjoying a gradual, graceful, and dignified end of life.

Keith D. Wisbaum, Esq.
Elder Abuse Attorney, Laguna Beach, Calif.

INTRODUCTION

We wrote this book for families

We wrote this book to give hope and encouragement to families and caregivers of the elderly. It feels like a lonely place, but you don't have to face the maze of elder care alone. While each family must take responsibility for its own aging generation, there are areas of common ground which, when shared, can lighten the load. We've been where you are. The two of us have experienced many years of overseeing and hands-on elder care in our own families, and advocacy for others in similar situations. Those years have provided us with practical, creative problem-solving experience. Let us help you cope with the monotony of the daily care or the sudden trauma of the unexpected crisis.

We wrote this book for the public

Abuse of the elderly does happen, not only in private homes, but also in all kinds of facilities for long-term care. That it happens at all is shocking; that it happens with such frequency is an appalling national disgrace. Every person in the nation and in the world faces the prospect of growing old and perhaps frail. We cannot assume that "it won't happen to me." Awareness and preparation and proactive involvement in one's own future can go far toward safeguarding that future.

We wrote this book for professionals

From years of dialogue with other advocates, medical professionals, long-term care industry managers, legal advocates, and legislators, we offer creative solutions to problems, from the standpoint of both the professionals and the families involved in elder care. There are measures that professionals can initiate and steps that families can encourage. Cooperative effort can ensure a better future for all of us.

PROLOGUE

Are you aware that we in the United States of America bear a national disgrace? Would you believe that grandmas are being beaten? Would you be outraged if your grandpa had a leg amputated because of a neglected bedsore? Or that your aunt had to go to a psychiatric facility for detoxification because she was overmedicated in a long-term care facility? Or that your mom was left alone all night in a wheelchair in the recreation room of another facility?

What would it take to convince you that these things are happening with frightening frequency all across our country? Would it have to happen to someone you love?

I wasn't aware of it. Then it happened to my Mom. I wanted it never to happen to anyone else. I had to do something. All I knew to do was tell her story.

~:~

Bessie Lane was a survivor. She faced life head-on with optimism, warmth, and love. She was a woman of her times, a woman of modesty and dignity — she was a lady.

Bessie was born February 26, 1897, one of seven children of working-class parents. Though times were often difficult, she was raised in an era when people did what they had to do. When her father's affluent but childless brother and his wife offered to help the family by taking one of the children into their home, sixteen-year-old Bessie was chosen.

Bessie not only survived the separation from her family, she thrived in the genteel atmosphere of her aunt and uncle's home. She finished her schooling and entered Uncle Charlie's business as hostess of Lane's Confectionery. Her lifelong love of sweets began during this time. No matter how many she tasted, strawberry ice cream remained her favorite.

Bessie met her handsome, kilted Scot at a church costume ball where she was Miss Liberty. Before he shipped overseas in World War I, David Jarvis proposed to her. She survived the loneliness of his absence. When he returned home safely, courting resumed, and on September 24, 1920, Bessie Lane married David.

Bessie survived those lean pre-depression years, creating their first home: one room with a shared bath in a house divided into apartments. She cooked on a one-burner hot plate, juggling pans to get everything hot at the same time. When their son, David, was born, Bessie negotiated for a larger apartment. Six years later a daughter, Betty Lane, was born, and they found a house more suited to their growing family.

Besides nurturing her own and all the neighborhood children, Bessie had a quick mind for business. When a neighbor needed to follow her husband in a job transfer, Bessie boldly offered $200 as a down payment on their house. The two women shook hands and settled the deal. Bessie had quite an announcement over dinner that evening. Their family was made complete with the arrival of Diane, their third child. Then came years of involvement in the children's school and church activities, overseeing studies, sewing, baking the homemade after-school treats — cookies, doughnuts, or cream puffs — making do with limited resources.

The onset of World War II demanded another kind of survival. There were sleepless nights as her only son marched off to serve in the army. Those years took their toll, but Bessie survived.

She survived the empty nest, joyfully welcoming new family members and the arrival of grandchildren.

"Of course, I'm not a bit proud of my grandchildren," she would say to any who would listen, beaming her approval like a benediction.

Years later, Bessie survived the loss of her beloved son when a heart attack felled him in the prime of life. Bessie survived by looking ahead with hope. But hope faltered when Bessie lost her dear Dave after more than sixty years of marriage. Yet, a few years later, her first great-grandchild was on the way.

Bessie Lane Jarvis was gentle, but tough — a product of her history. She was a lady. She was a survivor.

But she never rocked that first great-grandchild.

After ninety-one years, there was one thing Bessie could not survive....

1 ONE NIGHT'S NIGHTMARE

The shrill ringing knifed through my sleep. It was the night supervisor at the nursing home where Mom was a resident, calling to tell me Mother had unexplained bruises on her face. I was concerned, but not terribly worried. Mom often bumped her legs or arms on her bed or wheelchair. Her thin skin bruised easily. I was sure the nursing home was just being meticulous about reporting it to me.

At eight-thirty the phone rang again.

"Mrs. Sandell, I just needed to tell you the aide has been suspended."

"What do you mean? What happened? Never mind, I'll be right there."

I drove to the nursing home, replaying that phrase: The aide has been suspended — the aide has been suspended....

At the nursing home, I put a smile on my face as I stepped through the door into Mom's room. I reeled as if I'd been slapped. There lay Mom, ninety-one years old, eighty-five pounds, upper body restrained in a posey — a vest-like garment used to restrain the wearer in bed or in a chair. The top of her head and forehead were bruised and purpling. The imprint of a hand darkened her cheek and temple. Her nose was bloody and there was a blood clot under one eye.

"Mom!" I meant to say it gently. It came out as a shriek.

She opened her eyes and tried to reach her hand to mine.

"Here's my little honey," she said, her voice a whisper.

"Mom," I said, "how did this happen? Who did this to you?"

She closed her eyes and shook her head.

"I don't know ...she was big ...I was scared..."

Every word seemed an effort. "Sometime in the night," she sighed. "I'm so tired. I'm glad you're here, honey."

Leaning down to adjust the blanket around her, I saw ugly bruises on her upper chest.

"You rest, Mom. I'll be right back."

At the nurses' station there was a sudden spurt of activity with charts and phones. No one would meet my eyes. I asked for Mother's doctor's number.

"Oh, we've talked with Dr. Tynan," said a nurse. "The X-rays came back negative. Nothing's broken."

"I need to speak with him now."

She dialed without further comment and handed the phone to me. I was surprised that Dr. Tynan, himself, answered. I told him I needed to have him see Mother.

"I'm out on the road today, Mrs. Sandell. I don't know that I'll be able to make it."

Not able! I hung up and immediately dialed a family friend, a physician who'd known Mother for years. He said he'd come as soon as his office closed at noon.

An aide pushing an empty wheelchair stopped by my side and murmured, "Do you know who did that to your mother?"

I told her how Mom had described the woman.

"Oh!" said the aide. "I'm not surprised." Then she went on with her errand.

Not surprised? I turned back to the desk, my head reeling with the overload of information I'd taken in.

"This thing obviously happened in the night. Why did you wait until eight before calling me? And why wasn't I told about the aide until the second call at 8:30?"

"It was reported when the day shift was coming on, Mrs. Sandell. And we wanted to see that she was treated — "

I spun away from the desk. It occurred to me that perhaps they wanted the aide off the premises before I arrived. *It's probably a good thing I didn't see her,* I thought darkly. But I would like to have asked her, simply, "Why?"

I called my husband, Jim, and then my friend, Sue, who urged us to take photographs right away. A call home for the camera and film. Suddenly I thought of my sister, Betty Lane, in Pennsylvania. How could I tell her that our mother had been beaten in the night and that I had absolutely no answers? When I choked out the words, Betty offered to come right away, but we agreed it would be best for her to wait until we knew more. My mind cried, *What more is there to know? It happened!*

Sue arrived. While we stood by Mom's bed waiting for Jim, the nursing home administrator came in with a nurse. She walked to the bed, glanced down at Mother, and said brusquely, "That's too bad." Then she strode out of the room, without a word of explanation, apology, or comfort — literally without even acknowledging my presence. I was stunned.

When Jim and our daughter, Kathy, arrived, there were all the explanations again, and then the photos. How could I photograph this obscenity against a woman to whom dignity was a way of life?

Later, in the hall, an aide stopped me and whispered, "Mrs. Barton told me she heard what happened last night. She'll talk with you if you want. She's in the activities room."

I found Mrs. Barton, a tiny, frail, white-haired woman. When I told her who I was, she glanced around the room furtively. I sensed her vulnerability.

"What can you tell me, Mrs. Barton?" I asked as gently as I could.

"I know what time it was," she said. "I was awake. It happened twice, and I looked at my clock each time. It was at 11:30 last night, and again at one o'clock this morning."

Twice! I saw again those purple bruises that will remain forever in my memory.

"I heard slapping sounds," Mrs. Barton went on, shivering, "and your mother yelled out, 'Please, don't hit me anymore! Why are you hitting me?' And at one o'clock I heard her cry, 'Don't do that. It hurts. Please, don't hit me anymore!'" Mrs. Barton covered her face with her hands.

"You're sure of the times?"

"Oh, yes. There was enough light from the hall to see."

"Thank you, Mrs. Barton." I saw again how very frail she was. She seemed to wilt.

"I'm so sorry," she went on. "I should have called someone. I just couldn't."

I suddenly realized she was frightened for herself. How many others might have heard, but had been afraid to call for help? If Mother was screaming, why didn't any of the nurses or the rest of the staff hear?

Our son-in-law, Jim, a police detective, arrived, and, at my request, called the police. We alerted the administrator to the fact that they were coming. She merely nodded. I told her I needed to see Mother's records. She flatly refused. I told myself that I would see those records.

When the police arrived, I felt relieved that it was now in their hands. They were very gentle with Mother, but in her fatigue she could offer no real answers to their questions. They took numerous photos of her injuries and spoke with several people on the staff.

The afternoon wore on. It didn't get any easier. Our friend, Dr. Nichols, came and examined Mother. He checked the medical records and, though appalled with the situation, he eased my anxiety about her immediate physical condition, but he was concerned about the potential emotional aftermath of her ordeal.

It was one of the hardest things I've ever had to do to walk out the door that evening to go home. Mother was sleeping peacefully, but I knew it would be a long, sleepless night for me.

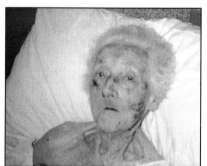

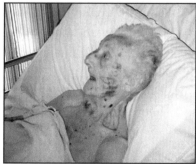

Bessie Jarvis—the morning after

"Here's my little honey... "
Black and blue and
bloodied—wondering why

2   TURN AROUND, TURN AROUND

Sunday was a typical hot California July day, but my spirit was frozen. I'd been wakeful all night, asking the same questions, replaying the events of the previous day. I had to move Mother to another nursing home. Although we were told the aide had been suspended, there was no acknowledgment that she was actually the perpetrator. What if it had been someone else, someone still on staff, someone who might retaliate?

As I hurried to the nursing home, my thoughts went back twenty-five years to the crises that brought Mom and Dad into our home for the rest of their lives.

It had been a perfect "White Christmas" day in Bowie, Maryland, in 1961. Mom was in a hospital recovering from gall bladder surgery, and Dad stayed in Baltimore to be with her. We were determined not to let undue concern about Mom's hospitalization dampen two-year-old Kathy's Christmas.

When the phone rang the next morning, it was my brother, Dave, calling to say that Dad had been in an accident Christmas night. A truck skidded on ice and broadsided Dad's car on his way home from visiting Mother. He was examined at the hospital and released, but fainted in the lobby, so was admitted for observation. It was determined that his spleen was damaged and might need surgery.

Both parents hospitalized! It was a tense time, juggling the needs of each, protecting each from worry about the other.

Though Dad didn't need surgery, Mom was released before he was. With both parents coming home, and neither able to care for the other, we brought them into our guestroom to recuperate. When we realized they'd need to live closer to family, we faced the painful task of dismantling their home in Baltimore — the house where I was born and lived till I married Jim — the house of a million memories.

We moved them into a little apartment near us, but it didn't work. Because of his injuries Dad couldn't go back to work and had to retire. Mom was having fainting spells. Dad couldn't cope. After several midnight trips to the rescue, pregnant and with our two-year-old in tow, we realized that if we were to be on twenty-four-hour call, it would be easier for all of us to be living under one roof.

We squeezed, creating a nest for five, knowing that before many months we'd be six when the new baby would arrive. As Mom and Dad got stronger and more confident in their new surroundings and status, they became a great team, helping run the household. Mom's fried chicken and potato salad became legendary; I looked forward to her night to cook. Dad became active in our church. A few months later our son, Mark, made his entrance. Mom and Dad had a new sense of security, and we had the support of live-in grandparents.

Mom loved being Granny. She had a gift, singing and rocking and loving both the baby and the toddler. The arrangement worked so well that in four subsequent business transfers, Mom and Dad moved with us, becoming a permanent part of our family, which grew to seven in 1969 when our youngest daughter, Kim, was born.

And now these arms that had reached out for hugs and offered love and cookies had tried, without success, to fend off hostile hands that had beaten her mercilessly.

Don't worry, Mom, I thought as I arrived at the nursing home. After checking on Mom, and requesting that she be moved closer to the nurses' station, I set out to find a new home for her. I scanned the list I'd made of facilities, wondering where to begin. I had chosen this nursing home with extreme care as the best available at the time. As I visited facilities on my list, I knew I was being paranoid, but I saw problems on every side. This one smelled, that one was dark, in another the residents were listless, in another the personnel unresponsive. But in addition to my requirements, there were other factors: the availability of space, and the fact that Mother would necessarily be a partial-pay resident (in California, Medi-Cal; other states, Medicaid), the kind for whom there were limited spaces. And finally, the personnel I spoke with seemed hesitant to talk with me after I told them Mother had been beaten. They seemed cold to her crisis.

"They haven't seen her," Jim said with his usual calm. "They're probably afraid you're exaggerating and will be paranoid about anything they do."

"Yes, I probably will," I responded.

Bessie and David Jarvis, in happier times

3 GET THE HELL OUT OF DODGE

Monday morning the halls of the nursing home bustled with normal activity, as if nothing had happened.

I learned that a doctor referred by Dr. Tynan had examined Mother and pronounced her "fine." I objected that a physician Mother didn't know had examined her, and that I hadn't been informed. It offended me that he said she was fine.

I found Mother shrunken and quiet, her searching, fearful eyes the most active thing about her. How could I reassure her when I had no control over who came and went, or what they might think it necessary to do to her? After sitting with her for an hour, trying to reassure her, trying to reassure myself that she was all right, I slipped out as she dozed.

I drove to pick up the photos we had taken. As awful as it had been to see her bruises on Saturday, I was unprepared for the graphic reality of the photos. The bruises were worse than I remembered. Cold rage coiled in my stomach.

Later, Kim and I were sitting with Mom when Dr. Tynan came in—his first visit since the incident. Dr. Tynan leaned down to look at Mother's face.

"That could have happened in a fall," he said, pointing to the bruise on her forehead. "And that one could have happened when they picked her up."

I almost laughed. *They pick them up by their faces?*

"No, Doctor," Kim said coldly. "She was beaten."

He didn't respond. I knew then that even though Mom was listed as his patient, he wasn't involved—didn't want to be involved. But it no longer mattered. I would move her as quickly as I could find a place.

The days that followed became a frustrating routine—doing things necessary to prepare for her move, yet not finding a satisfactory facility. I visited Mom at least twice a day; she was withdrawn and quiet. It became more difficult to go in, seeing her like that.

I wasn't satisfied to leave things as they were with Dr. Tynan. We had the right to certain expectations from a physician, even though he was under the umbrella of the facility provision. When I called to ask for an appointment, he immediately offered to withdraw from the case, but agreed to meet with me.

The next morning, when Doctor Tynan met me in the hospital lobby, I asked if we could speak somewhere privately. He steered me out onto the sidewalk. I had hoped for a more businesslike atmosphere — a desk, an office, a conference room — but so be it.

Always be a lady. Mother's frequent admonition echoed in my mind. Standing in the glaring morning sun, I thanked Dr. Tynan for seeing me, and explained the disappointment we felt that he hadn't thought it important to see Mother the day of her beating.

"She needed a physician she could rely on. We did too."

Dr. Tynan just looked at me. I think he was surprised there wasn't more. Finally he said, "I'm sorry I disappointed you." Then he turned and went back into the hospital.

By Friday, two weeks after the beatings, I was no closer to finding a new facility, and was running out of possibilities. I'd visited all the homes on my list, but couldn't bring myself to choose one. Finally, I was given the number of a highly recommended facility I hadn't previously heard of. Though it was late Friday afternoon, and the facility was on the far side of the county, I went to look at it.

There was a soothing, unhurried cordiality about Meg Stuckey, director of admissions. I immediately felt at ease, telling my story and showing her Mom's photos. There was an atmosphere about the place that instilled comfort and confidence. I'd have transferred Mom that evening, but we decided on Monday morning so the full staff would get the briefing on her care. I slept well for the first time since the incident, knowing there was an end in sight.

When we arrived at the nursing home on Monday morning, I was surprised, but relieved, to see Mother dressed and ready, waiting in a wheelchair, a lap robe tucked around her legs. Kim and I loaded her clothing and personal items into Kim's car and came back to wait for the ambulance I had requested. But I discovered that no ambulance had been ordered; there would be a ninety-minute wait and a $200 fee.

"Forget it!" I said abruptly to the nurse. "We'll take her ourselves."

What I really wanted to say was, "I just want to get the hell out of Dodge," an old family joke about escaping unpleasantness. But that didn't fit Mother's picture of a lady.

Kim and I wheeled Mom out to my car and struggled to get her into the front seat. I had brought pillows to cushion her in the ambulance, so I plumped them all around her, forming a padded nest. I tucked the lap robe around her knees and brought the seat belt across her lap and shoulders.

I locked the car door and turned to speak to Kim about the route to the new facility. An aide came out to return the wheelchair. She looked at me blankly.

"You know," she said sullenly, "we really did take very good care of her here."

4 | OVER THE RIVER AND THROUGH THE WOODS

I was aware of Kim's restraining hand on my arm, her eyes wide and dark as she watched the aide retreat through the nursing home door.

"Come on, Mom, let's just get out of here."

We pulled out of the parking lot in tandem. Mother started to get agitated, flailing her arms and hands. I tried to hold one hand and stroke it without taking my eyes off the road.

"Remember how we used to take rides, Mom?" It occurred to me that this could well be Mother's last car ride. "We'd laugh and sing," I said as gaily as I could. "Let's sing, Mom. 'Over the river and through the woods, to Grandmother's house we go.'"

Maybe not the best choice of songs. "You're going to have a new house, Mom — Granny. Won't that be great? You'll like it there. Things will be all right now...." I realized I was praying they would.

"Down beside the beautiful sea, that's where the children love to be.... Remember how you liked to go to the seashore in Maryland, Mom? Come on, Mom, sing with me. I think when I read that sweet story of old, when Jesus was here among men, how He called little children as lambs to His fold..."

Always songs about children. She loved the little ones so. An urgent honking startled me. I glanced in the rearview mirror and saw that Kim, in the car behind, was motioning me forward. I wondered how long the signal had been green. At least Mother was calmer now.

Finally we arrived at the new facility. I was exhausted. I'd been crying and needed to blow my nose! I mopped my face with a tissue and went inside.

"We've been expecting you," Meg Stuckey greeted me. "Bring your car right around by the side door and I'll have someone meet you. Her room is ready."

Mother was soon tucked into her new surroundings. Exhausted from all the activity, she fell asleep. Kim and I straightened things in her new dresser and sat by her bed most of the afternoon. Every time Mom stirred, I'd reassure her she was in her nice new home.

I soon saw how dedicated and caring the staff at the new facility really were. Recognizing Mom's fear, the director of nursing asked the entire staff to cooperate in a program to instill trust. She requested everyone who passed Mother's door to look in and call out "Hello," and call her by name. No one was to go near her or touch her except the aides and nurses who cared for her needs. Because of her many bruises and increasing lack of movement, a special bed with a heated water mattress was ordered. This was very soothing to her; she would lie on her side and stroke the mattress, feeling the water move beneath her fingers.

Despite the flowers and treats I brought every day, Mother seemed unresponsive. Sometimes she asked me where her mother was; sometimes she called me "Mother." I tried to correct her, but that agitated her. If she felt more peaceful calling me "Mother," why not?

Her bruises were healing; I hoped her psyche was as well. Mother often had bruises on her arms and legs at the old nursing home, and the reasonable explanation was that the elderly have such fragile skin it sometimes bruises, even in the needed frequent turning of the person in bed. It was also suggested that residents often accidentally bruise themselves in moving about. This can be true, but Mother had been here only two weeks and the marks on her body were nearly gone, though she was being turned even more frequently because of her diminished capacity to turn herself. Yet there was no new bruising.

It wasn't all perfect. Fear injected itself again when the administrator informed me that Mother had been yelling a lot, especially at night, disturbing other residents. If she continued being disruptive, she might have to be transferred to a secured facility. I knew "secured" was a euphemism for "locked." I'd seen some locked facilities. It didn't occur to me to ask why she, who couldn't walk or even get out of bed, would need to be in one.

I knew she'd been noisy at the other nursing home. She would call out or clap her hands loudly when no one responded to her need for the bathroom. She often had "accidents" while waiting. She was even considered combative, but her most basic needs were being ignored because she was considered "difficult." This was an affront to her dignity. Finally, she had been fighting for her life. No amount of noisiness or combativeness excused the lack of care or the beatings that occurred in the nursing home that had contracted to care for her.

I knew the administrator needed to see the photos. As he looked at them, his face reflected a new understanding of what Mother had been through. There was no further talk of moving her.

Mom became increasingly unaware and unresponsive, sleeping most of the time and confused when she was awake. Still, I visited with her as if she understood every word. One Thursday several weeks after we'd transferred her, I walked into her room with a heavy heart.

"Here's my honey, Di!" exclaimed the wraithlike figure in the bed.

"Mom!" I cried, rushing to kiss her, trying not to hug too vigorously. She clung to my hand as if she'd just returned from a long trip — maybe she had.

"Have you had lunch, Mom?" I was always trying to get food into her. "How about some ice cream?"

"Are we celebrating, honey?" Mom's eyes were sparkling.

"Absolutely! Would you like to have a birthday party?"

"With strawberry ice cream?"

"With strawberry ice cream!" My eyes suddenly filled with tears. I stumbled into the hall and stopped the first aide I saw.

"Please," I said, as if grasping for a lifeline. "I need a dish of strawberry ice cream. Right now! Please!" Within minutes she brought a large dish full.

I laughed and cried as I spooned mouthful after mouthful into Mother's eager lips. And we sang! I sang Happy Birthday to her, and she sang Happy Birthday to me. We sang all her old favorites. Even Christmas carols.

She ate the whole dish of ice cream.

"What a party," she smiled contentedly. "Thanks, honey."

Weary from the exertion, she soon drifted to sleep and I went home, drained but happy. I was eager to see her the next day. I arrived with flowers and candy and the latest letter from Betty Lane, but Mom was asleep. I left, disappointed. Jim was quick to recognize my emptiness and offered to postpone our scheduled dinner out, but I thought we all might benefit from being waited upon.

It was a lovely evening. We found lots to talk about, and it seemed good to just relax and enjoy one another. We laughed a lot.

When we got home at nine o'clock, the phone was ringing.

Mother had just passed away.

My Mom is very special, God, hear my whispered prayer,
I miss her very much You know, There's sadness everywhere.

"I know, I know, my child, I'll wipe away your tears.
It's time for her to be with Me, you've had her many years.

"She's oh, so happy home with Me, My special loving guest,
She wanted peace and comfort, and yes, some needed rest.

"Diane, your mom is singing, her voice raised up in praise,
Your dad was there to greet her, they're together all the days.

"Your mom and dad are with Me in everything they do, and
We'll be here — we promise, when your life on earth is through."

Oh Lord, I feel much better, and I love You very much,
I need You close beside me, I need Your loving touch.
I miss her, so my tears will flow —

"I know — it's good to cry, I'll stay close by and hold you
And pat each teardrop dry."

— Ann Simons, for Bessie Jarvis, 1988

5 5/3 TURKEY

Are we ever really ready to say goodbye to a parent? Even if they've been very ill; even if they've become someone we don't know; even if their "quality of life" has no quality as we see it? Jim's parents were both gone; my dad had died four years before. Now Mom. Suddenly I felt very alone, my roots gone. And yet I felt relief. And then guilt for the relief. It took a long time to realize both feelings were natural. I was relieved Mom's struggles were over. I thought, mistakenly, that mine were too.

"Remember, Diane, always be a lady."

"Turkey," Jim used to call her, teasing.

"You're the turkey," she'd give right back. She'd adored him from the time he was fifteen years old.

When we arrived at the facility, we were told Mother awoke after I left, and had eaten a very good dinner. *That's good,* I thought. *She always insisted on a good meal before leaving on a trip.*

They'd found her, peacefully gone, at bedtime rounds.

I wept, wishing I'd been there when she awoke that afternoon. But I was grateful for the wonderful day before, and thankful, too, that all her bruises were totally healed.

When she went into the other nursing home, she was Bess Jarvis, a lady. They turned her into someone else. The new facility had given her back to us as much as they were able.

The mortuary assistant appeared at the doorway.

"I'll stay," I said, holding Mother's hand.

"It may be difficult for you," he said.

"I need to be with her, especially now. You will be very gentle with her," I said, pleading.

"Yes, of course I will."

"That's to go along with her," I said, nodding at the soft new teddy bear Kim had tucked in her arm.

"Certainly." He smiled as if every ninety-one-year-old lady made her final ride with a teddy. "I need to close now, if you want to step out."

"No, I'll stay." I patted Mother's arm one more time before he zipped the body bag shut.

Goodbye, Mom....

I walked with him to the side door where the others were waiting, the same door we'd brought Mother in four weeks earlier. When the hearse started to pull away, the attendant rolled down the window.

"I'll be very careful with her, Mrs. Sandell."

Goodbye, Mother ...good-bye ...5/3....

Mother had chosen to be cremated, as had Dad years before. It was no easier this time, but at least I knew what to do, what to expect. On the appointed morning for the aerial distribution of ashes over the ocean, the pilot had told us he would buzz the pier where we stood, then circle around and fly straight out over the pier into the horizon to the three-mile limit before scattering her ashes.

"She's on her way to Pop," I said, clinging tightly to Jim's arm as the little plane shot into the shimmering autumn light above the waves. We dropped a yellow rose into the water and watched it float.

"She's at peace now. No more hurts. No more tears. Goodbye, Mom...."

The healing had begun.

We found a restaurant with outdoor tables and had a quiet lunch. We toasted Mom with a glass of wine.

Goodbye, Mother ...5/3...

A few weeks later, Betty Lane came from Pennsylvania, and we had a memorial service celebrating Mom's life. It gave not only her family, but her extended, adopted "family" of friends and neighbors who had gone through this trauma with us, an opportunity to reclaim the happy memories, the real person behind the battered shell we'd seen at the last.

Thornton Wilder said, "The highest tribute to the dead is not grief but gratitude." So many things to be grateful for ...All the memories ...her love of family, children, babies, flowers and lovely things...Christmas...Grandpa putting the hooks in all the ornaments, Granny by his side, diligently supervising where we were to hang each ornament...Grandma, not the kids, always the first one up on Christmas mornings, waking us all with the call that Santa had come...crisp new dollar bills in crisp white envelopes marked $XOXOX$ ... 5/3....

Of course, I'm not very proud of them...of course, I don't love them very much...

And don't forget...always be a lady....

We sang all her favorite hymns and some of the old children's songs she loved.

Goodbye, Mom...know that you've left us smiling...5/3.

After the service, we hosted a "celebration" supper at our home. In the family tradition for any occasion of merit, we had a champagne toast. Jim capped the evening.

"We always teased Granny about her fondness for champagne. At any party or event I filled her glass first, but by the time I'd get around the room to all the rest, Granny's glass would be empty and she'd hold it up for more. So, Granny, have a toast with Pop tonight. Here's to you, turkey! We love you — 5/3."

5/3 was Bessie's private code for the extra-special granny-sized love she had for her children and grandchildren.

6 Tip of the Iceberg

To live with the fact of Mother's death, I had to realize something positive from it. I determined to tell her story to everyone who would listen, so that no other frail old person would have to experience the terror and pain she had borne.

Telling Bessie's story in many different ways led to a variety of media opportunities, from the local newspaper, to a national magazine, to local and national radio and TV appearances, to an interview with Mrs. Barbara Bush at the White House. Each presentation led to contacts with others who'd experienced similar horrors. The resulting letters and phone calls further confirmed that I wasn't alone. Extracted from my case histories as an advocate, the material in this chapter is reported collectively in order to substantiate the scope of elder abuse throughout the US. These instances of abuse and/or neglect (which constitutes abuse) represent examples from hundreds of cases from thirty-eight states.

Reliable statistics on elder abuse don't exist for several reasons. It's very difficult to prove. In recent years more media attention has been given to elder abuse; however, many instances focus on abuse in the home by a relative or hired caregiver. While there may be no witnesses to the abuse in the home, the physical evidence and symptoms, as well as the presence and opportunity of the responsible person, often lead to prosecution.

The same kinds of abuse, with the same physical evidence and symptoms, in long-term care facilities can be nearly impossible to prove because so many caregivers are on the premises and so many plausible explanations are offered. If there's no eyewitness, there's seldom a fixing of responsibility.

Many incidents of abuse are unreported. Fragile residents fear retribution. Even when the abuse is against another, a witness may fear for his or her own safety. There is lack of recognition of what abuse really is.

Aides don't always recognize signs of abuse, or fear losing their jobs if they report. Physicians don't always recognize abuse, incorrectly offering other reasons for physical evidence, which is often dismissed as natural bruising of aging skin or as resulting from a fall or bumping into furniture or doors. Physicians and care facilities are mandated reporters by law. Since the original publication of this book, some facilities have incorporated training programs for recognition of signs of abuse. Families can be in denial, thinking such things couldn't possibly happen, or not wanting to face the problems associated with confrontation. They fear retaliation for "rocking the boat." Many elders without family or friends to help them fear having to leave a familiar setting — even a hurtful one — if they complain. Many don't know how to register a complaint, or even that it's an option. The scarcity of affordable facilities makes finding a new one a formidable task.

Everywhere I told my story, people confirmed that they too had experienced problems with long-term care facilities. Consider that I'm one person, founder of one advocacy nonprofit organization. Consider the untold numbers of other family members and advocates and organizations nationwide. Consider the added factor of unreported abuse. When these incalculable numbers are considered, the picture of the iceberg is not unrealistic. There may never be a reliable method of verifying the magnitude of this problem, but it's very real, very frightening, and very widespread. Los Angeles City Councilman Joel Wachs has repeatedly termed it a "national disgrace."

Here is just a sampling of incidents of abuse and/or neglect from my files.

- Neglect of decubitis ulcers (bedsores) led to infection, sepsis, gangrene, death.

- Resident thirsty, requests ignored, water consistently out of reach, led to dehydration, emergency hospitalization.

- Obstructive mass in neck, noted on admission record; discrepancy in facility records, and physician's records; records re-dated; resident died, malignant mass.

- Unattended resident fell from bed, cried for help, was found in respiratory distress; inadequate care contributed to the death of another resident that shift.

- As "punishment" for calling out, resident was left overnight in wheelchair in dark activities room, dressed only in gown.

- Facility failed to provide necessary diabetic diet, insulin administered improperly, insulin overdose, dehydration and death.

- Resident was yelled at, pinched, and later beaten by male aide who was bathing her.

- Residents with urine, feces, and vomit on their clothes.

- Forty-five-minute delay in answering call bells; wounds treated with non-sterile gloves.

- Resident observed naked beneath open dressing gown; later reported missing, picked up by two youths in a truck, deposited in a neighboring town.

- Resident reported missing; not found in search of premises; later found lying at foot of a little-used stairway.

- Immobile victim of multiple sclerosis burned by broken light fixture that fell (damaged fixture had been previously reported by relative).

- Bowel blockage, treatment delayed, resident sent to hospital, bowel exploded, patient died.

- Diabetic resident was treated as stroke victim, given medication to raise blood sugar, went into coma, died.

- Resident, left alone in chair in shower room, fell, became paralyzed from neck down.

- Resident's kneecap was shattered, resulting in amputation.

- Many reports of infected bedsores, some leading to amputations, some to death.

- Many reports of rough treatment, pinching, slapping, verbal abuse, threats, indignities, disregard of privacy, rape.

- Many personal items stolen, gift packages undelivered.

- Many reports of neglected bedding changes: dried urine stains; dried embedded fecal matter.

- Many reports of water withheld "because of increased bed changes necessary."

- Many reports of inappropriate food for condition of resident; food placed out of reach; trays picked up too soon; food jammed into mouth.

Elder abuse does happen. That it happens at all is a tragedy. That it happens with frequency is a disgrace.

There seems to be no pattern regarding the victims. Residents whose families visit often are just as likely to be targets as those who have no family or advocate. But just imagine the plight of those who have no one to stand up for them.

Why does elder abuse happen?

- Lack of proper training and education of CNAs (certified nursing assistants), who do most of the handling of residents, with specific emphasis on geriatric issues and indoctrination;

- Too many residents to care for;

- Low wages, little recognition or dignity afforded CNAs, engendering low self-esteem;

- Language barrier: aides and/or residents sometimes speak limited English; different cultural standards; stress of job and of personal problems; working two shifts or two jobs; correct tone not demonstrated by administration of facility;

- Corporate management more concerned with bottom line than with the human element.

Finally, it must be mentioned that some residents themselves, through lack of understanding, personality changes, physical limitations, and lack of cooperation, may exhibit abusive behavior to their caregivers, resulting in abusive reaction. There is, however, no excuse whatsoever for any professional caregiver to retaliate. Nor is there any excuse for any facility to justify such actions.

7   THERE OUGHT TO BE A LAW

Everyone assumed I would sue the nursing home, but first on my mind was that the home's top-level management needed to know what had happened there. I found the name of the CEO on a piece of promotional literature, and phoned his office for an appointment. I was told they would get back to me.

It took seven months! And that was only after an open letter to every member of the board of directors, outlining the attempts I had made and the unsatisfactory responses from the corporate office. I requested a meeting with the entire board, but was finally granted an appointment with the CEO who also invited the president of long-term care, with whom I'd met months before.

In the meantime, before Mother died, I made inquiries of an attorney. I was interested only in the facility being held accountable for what had happened. I wasn't interested in money, but the attorney explained that award of compensation is what proves the principle. After looking at the photos, he felt there was definite basis for a suit, but that the time in the courts likely would be extensive, and the settlement not worth the investment.

After Mother died, I learned there was, at that time in California, no recourse against the facility whatsoever. This seemed the most incredible affront of all. The nursing home would not be held accountable for the merciless beatings! And I had no doubt that those beatings contributed to Mother's death.

Several months later, an *Orange County Register* article on nursing home investigations caught my attention. I called the reporter, Jane Glenn Haas. When I shared Mother's story, she asked if I'd be willing to talk with her for publication. The response to the subsequent article, by mail and by phone, triggered the realization that other people were experiencing similar situations.

On the phone one day, Marc Hankin introduced himself. An attorney with the Beverly Hills Bar Association, he had seen the article. He had long been interested in elder issues, and had recently drafted new legislation for California Senator Mello's office, which, had it been in effect, would have made a difference in Mother's case. He expected media coverage of the bill within a few weeks, and asked if I would consider appearing with him, as a family member who had experienced one of the very situations this bill would cover.

I knew now where I could help make a difference.

~:~

On October 9, 1991, Governor Pete Wilson signed California Senate Bill 679, The Elder Abuse and Dependent Adult Civil Protection Act, which allows the families of abused elders — even after death — to bring suit. It also provides, upon a favorable verdict, for remuneration of attorney's fees and court costs by the perpetrator, and for possible determination by the court of a monetary award to the family.

Because of a family trauma in his last year of law school, Marc Hankin has become a pioneering advocate in elderlaw. He created Assembly Bill 2615, Spousal Protection Against High Cost of Long Term Care, which asserts the rights of Medi-Cal applicants to separate their community property without divorcing. Thanks to this bill, California law now dictates the automatic and equal division of a couple's assets on the day either of them enters a nursing home. Only the nursing home resident's half must be spent down to qualify for Medi-Cal. Also, nursing homes have been required by law to inform patients and their families that their assets can be divided.

Even though my mother's abuse was investigated by the ombudsman's office, the local Department of Health Services, Licensing and Certification, the local police, the district attorney, and the office of the Attorney General of the State of California Medi-Cal Fraud Division, no one was charged. Not even the facility was held accountable, because no hard proof of abuse could be attributed to the perpetrator. That was unacceptable, so I went to the state-level Department of Health Services, Licensing and Certification in Sacramento (Calif.). As a result of their involvement, since July 1992, Title 22 of the California Code of Regulations, Section 72527, has been amended to require long-term care facilities to ensure that a resident's right to be free from mental and physical abuse is not violated. In other words, facilities are not only responsible for care, but also for the protection of the resident. It took four long years to win this determination, which would in turn protect others.

This is a step in the right direction, but without a means of identification, alleged perpetrators have been known to leave one facility and move to another. As of 1998, California has legislated fingerprinting requirements. Standardized fingerprinting requirements covering all staff of every type of care facility is needed throughout the United States. Why should we feel we've solved the problem by dismissing a suspected abuser, only to have him or her show up in the facility down the street?

Task force committees, made up of knowledgeable participants, can perform a valuable service by studying existing legislation, evaluating and proposing new or amended legislation, and coordinating efforts among legislators to network information and advocacy. We would like to see coordination and cooperation between states through legislators, the attorneys general, and even the governors.

There are laws, federal and state; there need to be more. The long-term care industry insists they are over-regulated, yet the lack of enforcement of laws and regulations, the loopholes, the waiving of fines, leave little incentive for compliance. And the abuse reports continue.

Carole Herman, president of FATE (Foundation Aiding the Elderly), located in Sacramento, California, writes in a 2006 report, *Nursing Homes ... Business As Usual:*

> In 1987, President Ronald Reagan signed into law the Omnibus Budget Reconciliation Act (OBRA), the first major version of federal standards for nursing home care since the 1965 creation of both Medicare and Medicaid (Medi-Cal in California). Long-term

care facilities wanting Medicare and Medicaid funding were to provide services so that each nursing home patient could attain and maintain the highest physical, mental, and psychosocial well-being. However, almost 20 years later, poor care and abuse are still too common an occurrence in the approximately 16,000 nursing homes in the United States.

One of FATE's services is filing complaints with the state regulatory agencies on behalf of nursing home, assisted living, residential care, and acute care hospital patients and residents. Some of these complaints result in the appropriate state department citing these facilities for violations of federal and state regulations.

The complaints listed in the *FATE Newsletter* (Vol. 5 No 1, Winter 2006), represent only some of the incidents dealt with by FATE — one advocacy organization in one reporting period. Unfortunately, these incidents are still of the same magnitude as the extensive list in chapter 6, collected for the first edition of this book in 2000! Herman concludes, twenty years later, that the condition of care in long-term facilities is "Business as Usual."

So, yes, there are laws, but unless we're aware of them and understand them, and unless they're enforced, laws can't guarantee the safety of our elders. As a starting point, we suggest the compilation of a printed guide outlining the basic laws currently in effect, in easily understood layman's terms. (Examples in California: *Nursing Home Companion: A User-Friendly Guide to Nursing Home Laws and Practices*, and *How to Get Care From A Residential Care Facility*, prepared by attorneys of Bet Tzedek Legal Services, Los Angeles). This would be an invaluable resource for all caregivers. Please see chapters 11 and 14 for further discussion of these issues.

No government action or agency, no advocacy or individual, can ensure the elderly against abuse. Each family must take responsibility for its own loved ones.

8 A National Disgrace

As the "builder generation" has reached retirement age, perception of the "golden years" has improved for many. Their work ethic and responsible savings, investments, and retirement plans have given many a purchasing power and quality of life undreamed of by their parents' "Great Depression" generation. Beautiful retirement communities all over the nation add to the impression that today's retirees have it made. But not all our senior generation enjoys that lifestyle.

Grandmas are beaten; grandpas have amputations due to neglected bedsores; aunts undergo detoxification because they've been overmedicated; moms are left alone to sit all night in wheelchairs — in the facilities contracted to care for them!

What would convince you that these abuses occur all across our nation with frightening frequency and a shameful years-long repetitive history? Must it happen to someone you love?

I wasn't aware of it until it happened to my mom. Then I became convinced. I wanted it never to happen to anyone else. I was given the opportunity to tell her story when I was invited to appear on *Inside San Diego* (San Diego, California). When the studio asked me to bring the abuse photos, I resisted, not wanting strangers to see Mother's injuries. But without graphic proof, it's too easy for those unfamiliar with elder abuse to dismiss its awful reality. I was torn until the night before the show, when a chance encounter with other guests at the motel settled the issue. My husband and I were relaxing in the Jacuzzi when a young couple and their little son joined us. In a hot tub, it's easy to drift into conversation, and ours led to Mother's story.

I was careful not to speak graphically in front of the little boy, but the father nodded in recognition. "My grandfather was hurt in a nursing home. It affected our whole family." As they left to take the boy to bed, the dad said he'd be watching the show before they checked out in the morning.

I decided then to tell Mother's story for the cameras — with photos. Before we left the studio there were phone calls. Once more, I knew that such abuse wasn't an isolated occurrence.

Marc Hankin soon called again to tell me we had been scheduled for *The Home Show,* broadcast out of Los Angeles. Marc would be explaining what the law could do to protect elders, and specifically the new proposed California Senate Bill 679. Because my story was a "case in point" that so perfectly fit the legislation, I was to share from the family's viewpoint.

This was nationwide television; I had imaginary nightmares about showing up with mismatched shoes, but the interview went well. I met Marc in person that morning for the first time. He and I were able to relax into the discussion, which went back and forth from my experience to Marc's proposed legislation.

A few weeks later he called again asking me to do a press conference at Los Angeles City Hall, announcing the city council's unanimous support for SB 679. I agreed. Councilman Joel Wachs had called the conference, and instead of just reading the motion of support, invited several people to share their stories, giving faces and details to the statistics. Five times during the news conference, he referred to the problem of elder abuse as "a national disgrace." It was the first time I had heard a government official use the term. I was filled with gratitude, respect, and new encouragement. We were given as much time as we wished to tell our stories. The media people were attentive and respectful.

The late Doris Winkler, at that time host of the nationwide *Senior Report*, a program featuring issues of interest to senior citizens, asked to interview me. In ensuing months Doris did several follow-up reports. I could always tell when one of the reports was aired, and in what part of the country, because my mailbox would overflow with mail from specific states where the show was broadcast.

I heard from and became friends with a personal advocate in Arkansas, and later was interviewed by Arkansas public service television.

Several times I was a guest of the late Morgan Williams on her radio show, *The Big Picture,* on KBIG in Los Angeles. As we were going through the voice testing, Morgan told me about being at her mother's side during a hospital stay. She said the long, noisy night in strange surroundings gave her an empathy with the fear that elderly people feel in unfamiliar situations.

Several years later, a freelance writer interviewed me for an article for *Family Circle* magazine's feature column, "Women Who Make a Difference."

All these appearances brought heartbreaking letters. I answered every one. These people felt they had nowhere to turn. Because I'd gone through it, I felt I could at least point them in the right direction. It seemed something I could do in Mother's memory.

One man was told he'd have to take his wife out of the hospital in three days. She'd been neglected in several nursing homes. He couldn't return her to any of those, and the others in the area were too distant for him to be able to visit. He was distraught. Because of the mail delivery, it was the last day by the time I received his letter. Hoping I could reach him, I picked up the phone and was relieved to be able to put him in touch with the local ombudsman. In a follow-up call I learned they had been able to find a satisfactory place for his wife.

Another letter came from a woman, elderly herself, whose mother, wearing only a light robe, had somehow wandered to the street in front of her nursing home. She was apparently picked up, driven to another town, and let out. The nursing home was dirty, rife with cockroaches, unwashed linens, unmade beds, vile smells, and neglected residents, but due to her own poor health she could not bring her mother home.

What kind of answer can you give a person in such a situation? People had no idea where to go for help. It wasn't that there were no agencies out there; people just didn't know where to go. I was convinced there was a big problem, one that was eating away at a whole generation of elders, as well as at their children who were their caregivers.

A national disgrace!

The following is a copy of the motion Los Angeles City Councilman Joel Wachs made in September 1991. It's included here as an example of the types of advocacy that can be accomplished by one person, one group, one city, in the war against abuse of our elderly.

MOTION
Presented to the Los Angeles (CA) City Council
By Joel Wachs, Councilman, 2nd District

It is a sad fact of American life that elderly and dependent adults are vulnerable to physical, psychological or other abuses on the part of family members or other caregivers — those who are stronger than, or have other means of control over them. Incidents of abuse continue to be reported in many different forms, including physical isolation, physical attacks, verbal intimidation and harassment, starvation, unhealthful living conditions, and theft.

In 1990, the House Aging Committee estimated that more than 1.5 million elderly Americans each year may be victims of physical or mental abuse, most frequently by family members. Furthermore, the incidence of elder abuse nationwide was found to have increased by 50% since 1980.

Various federal and State legislative proposals have been made to reduce elder abuse, including SB 679 (Mello), which, among other things, would authorize the courts to award to the plaintiff attorney's fees and costs, including the cost of a conservator, where it is proven by clear and convincing evidence that a defendant is liable for physical abuse, neglect or fiduciary abuse of an elder or dependent adult and that the defendant has been guilty of recklessness, oppression, fraud or malice in the commission of abuse. The intent of this bill is to create additional incentives for attorneys to represent the victims of abuse, as well as to discourage acts of egregious abuse.

I THEREFORE MOVE that the City support SB 679 (Mello) and/or similar legislation which would authorize the award of attorney's fees and costs when it is proven by clear and convincing evidence that the defendant has been guilty of recklessness, oppression, fraud or malice in the commission of abuse.

UNANIMOUSLY APPROVED SEPTEMBER 4, 1991.

9   WE GO PUBLIC

Because of the response to the media appearances, I was in a continual state of agitation. The desperation in these contacts demanded response. I knew there were ways of getting attention and action, ways of solving problems and redirecting the hurt and frustration. Despite my empathetic indignation, I recognized that real healing was taking place for me as well, because I could see how to pass along to others what I had learned. Their concerns were today and needed attention today. My situation was past; nothing could change it. The door was closed for Bessie Jarvis, but was ajar on the future — a future dark with national shame unless we could turn the situation around.

An advocate I'd spoken with gave me a great gift. "I believe you. I understand," were her first words to me, and as I spoke with more and more people about their experiences, I was able to pass that gift along. "I believe you. I understand."

When we've experienced the abuse of an elder loved one, so many voices try to dissuade us from the word "abuse." By the industry and even from medical personnel, we have been told, "No, no, he fell!" "Oh, but she's always bumping into things." "Their skin is so fragile, you know." "Don't you know how difficult he is to deal with?" From casual observers we hear, "Surely, you misunderstood." "I've never heard a bad report about that place." From some corners we hear, "Don't make so much of it." "Aren't you being obsessive about this?"

But from those who've endured the helpless heartbreak of the abuse of an elder loved one, their pain is proof enough. There is only acceptance and "I believe you. I understand."

The frustration and helplessness expressed in the calls and mail convinced me of the need for an advocate for the victims of abuse and their families. My advocacy became centered on helping the families. My guestroom quickly filled up with letters, files, news clippings, and supportive literature. The early correspondence was all handwritten; I couldn't type. As the workload increased, I called a friend with whom I had done volunteer work in the past, to offer the position of "Volunteer Executive Secretary." She was often seen crawling around the guestroom on her hands and knees, searching out information from the files.

Friends and family urged me to make the advocacy official; thus NOBLE (Network Outreach Better Living for the Elderly) was born, and incorporated as a nonprofit grassroots corporation, complete with a board of directors that met around my dining room table. Our stated purpose was to make people aware of the existence of, and potential for, abuse and neglect of the elderly in long-term care facilities, and to initiate action to improve eldercare. The name NOBLE derived from ways to accomplish the goals: networking, disseminating information, and outreach, resulting in better living for the elderly. Mother would have loved the name; Noble had also been my brother's middle name. We hoped that the searing flame of Bessie's pain and ours would light the torch of hope through education of others.

I began to tell our story to groups, classes, service clubs, and philanthropic organizations. I related my background and history, and from that, my knowledge of the issues. My conclusions, advice, and recommendations were always prefaced with, "If it were my mother or father…."

The First Presbyterian Church of Orange responded to hearing about our guestroom office situation by offering us an office rent-free. In an indirect but very tangible way, they were ministering to the elderly, and I certainly felt I was part of their mission outreach. A local business donated beautiful new office furniture. The volunteer staff expanded through the generosity of friends and church members. My time was also unpaid. I was a CEO with no salary, no car, no professional wardrobe, and no expense account, but I couldn't give up. Word was getting out that we were available. The number of people who found us in the telephone book surprised even me.

Networking came about by our involvement with other agencies and groups. I chaired California State Senator John Lewis' Task Force for the

Elderly. I recommend such committees as an excellent way to acquire and disseminate information and influence action. We were able to help families tell their stories in a wider forum as well as help the senator and his colleagues better understand the reality of the problem. (See chapter 14 and appendix H for details on task forces and cooperating with government representatives for improved eldercare conditions.)

Because I'd learned the value of networking, I assumed several additional roles in conjunction with the work of NOBLE. I sat on the boards of directors of the Orange County Council on Aging — Ombudsman, and of FATE (Foundation Aiding the Elderly) in Sacramento, California. I served on two other committees: the Long-term Care Consumer Advocates of the State Licensing and Certification Committee, Sacramento, and the Alzheimer's Association Public Policy Committee of Orange County. In each of these the reciprocal benefits of exchange of information, suggestions, and resources resulted in a growing pool of help for elders and their families.

NOBLE created and maintained a library of resources, as well as schedules of classes, seminars, and workshops to which we often sent representatives. We also obtained information regarding resources, services, and advocacies in other states, from which clients could get help, and from which I could get resources for callers from other states.

We visited long-term care facilities throughout the area to keep aware of conditions. We made it a policy never to recommend facilities; that had to be a family's decision. But we were available to accompany families when they were trying to resolve problems in facilities or with agencies such as Licensing. From just such instances we created the Five-point Plan for evaluating eldercare and resolving problems (discussed in chapter 15 and appendix F).

Despite the generous provision of office space, funding for operation was always difficult. There was never a cost to clients or families requesting help, and I never asked a fee for speaking to groups. Most of our funds were donated by friends and relatives, organizations to which I'd spoken, and occasionally by families whom we had helped. Recognition awards in 1992 and 1993 from the Soroptimist International of Orange, and a Disneyland Community Service Award in 1994, came as surprise boosts to the budget, but regular funding was extremely difficult to find. As widespread as the problem is, and as vital as the work of solving it is, our society is in denial about it. Therefore we don't fund to solve the problem.

Because of lack of funding, NOBLE had to close its doors for a while. But because of opportunities and circumstances that have arisen in the years since, NOBLE reopened shortly before the original publication of this book in 2000, and is currently headquartered in Knoxville, Tennessee, providing services throughout many states. You can access information about NOBLE at www.NOBLEusa.org.

NOBLE was a gift to me. It provided the means to an end: closure of Mother's "chapter."

NOBLE was her gift to others. It provided families the means to address and solve their own problems, and ultimately to find closure.

The need is still strong. The problem of elder abuse is not solved. Everywhere I go I still meet people who are experiencing problems and don't know where to turn. Other advocates report the same situation. I still tell the story, still try to help. This book carries forward the purposes and goals of NOBLE — To advocate "Better Living for the Elderly."

10 MEETING MILLIE AND MRS. BUSH

Diane Sandell with Mrs. Barbara Bush
Photo by Carol Powers/White House Photographer

In NOBLE's quest to make the public aware of the danger to our nation's senior population, I had appeared on several TV and radio shows, and was receiving mail from all over the United States confirming that my experience wasn't an isolated event. The potential for elder abuse touches virtually every family in the nation and in the world. Barring catastrophic illness or accidental death, we will all face the challenges of growing old. Until people realize and accept the fact that this is a universal problem that affects them personally, they tend to dismiss the subject. I hoped to enlist a highly visible, credible spokesperson to help spread the message. Informed awareness will go far in helping to curb and solve this national disgrace.

I wrote to high-profile people: government officials, local, state, and nationwide, whose attention and sponsorship of legislation could make a difference; media personalities who present social issues in formats seen by millions; movie and TV actors who'd appeared in stories about issues facing the elderly; and the First Lady, Mrs. Barbara Bush. After an initial inquiry to Mrs. Bush's office, I had been sending updates of my work for her information and files. Randa Mendenhall had assured me of Mrs. Bush's interest and appreciation, and invited me to continue submitting materials and information.

Throughout the following months, I had frequent calls from Ms. Mendenhall on Mrs. Bush's behalf. It became a family joke between the kids as they'd call me to the phone: "It's the White House again, Mom."

In spring 1992, *Family Circle* magazine published a bit of our story in their feature column, "Women Who Make A Difference." Although I was disappointed that the coverage had to be limited to fit the feature format, it was exciting to see references to our advocacy in print. I had developed a great rapport with Ms. Mendenhall, and felt that in her I had found a caring friend and a valuable advocate, so I phoned her to say that the magazine was on the stands. She assured me she'd get a copy.

Randa called again later. After reading the article, Mrs. Bush inquired if it might be advisable to set up a meeting with me on some future trip to California. I responded that I planned to be on the East Coast in June, and would be delighted to schedule a meeting at her convenience.

Finally, June arrived, and my sister and I were visiting her friend in Washington.

Although I had appointments with several advocates in Washington, I hadn't contacted or heard from Randa since our arrival. We were lunching at Union Station when our hostess called her home and learned that the White House had called trying to locate me. When I immediately called Randa, she got right to the point.

"We've been trying to reach you. Mrs. Bush had wanted to meet with you today, but ..."

"Does that mean it's not going to happen?" I asked, with sinking heart.

"Actually, no. She offered an alternate time, and could meet with you at noon tomorrow, if you're — "

"I'm free!"

"Guess what!" I said as I returned to the table. "We're going to the White House tomorrow!"

We made appointments to have our hair done first thing the next morning, and spent the rest of the afternoon like schoolgirls discussing our wardrobe options. That evening I received phone calls from various aides with instructions explaining what to expect, procedures, and security checks. Although I had known I'd be allowed to bring my sister, it was a generous bonus that I could invite our hostess.

I spent a restless night, projecting all my concerns and questions onto the day ahead. It dawned on me that I didn't know how much time had been allotted for our visit. I knew this would be my only chance to share my concerns face to face, and though I was experienced in giving two-hour seminars, I realized I'd be fortunate to have only five or ten minutes with the First Lady. I refined my story to the most vital essence possible.

We received an early call confirming the noon appointment with Mrs. Bush. We trooped to the beauty salon for fresh hairdos. We were going to meet the First Lady!

At the first gate it was exhilarating to tell the uniformed guard we had an appointment with Mrs. Bush. After checking his list, he passed us through to the second gate where we were met by another guard with a formidable-looking German shepherd that inspected the car and the trunk. Passed through to where we should park, we walked to the third gate where a guard checked all our identification. Then it was through the metal detectors.

We were getting closer! Just inside the portico, a gentleman rose from behind a mahogany desk and ushered us into a waiting room. A woman stepped through the door and said, "I'm Randa." Although we'd never seen each other before, we instinctively hugged. We were escorted upstairs to an office where we met other volunteers and staff.

"May I take pictures?" Betty Lane asked, indicating her camera.

"Oh, Mrs. Bush has arranged for the White House photographer to take pictures."

We were then taken into the China Room, where the china from various administrations is displayed. A member of Mrs. Bush's staff entered and went through the protocol, explaining that Randa would introduce us to the First Lady. *We'll get five minutes at most,* I thought. We were escorted to the Diplomatic Reception Room, where heads of state are received.

Everything became silent. I turned to see Millie padding through the door, making the rounds, allowing each of us in turn to pet her. As we were all smiling and fussing over Millie, Mrs. Bush appeared in the doorway, followed by a Secret Service agent who quickly glanced around the room. The photographer materialized from somewhere and was already snapping pictures as Randa presented us to Mrs. Bush. She was indeed the First Lady of the land and of the White House, but the "lady of the house" as well. I felt like a friend, a guest in her home. I felt I could have invited her to tea in my own home.

"It's a pleasure to meet you, Mrs. Bush," I said. "I believe you know why I'm here, and what happened to my mother."

"Yes, I've seen the pictures."

This wasn't just a courtesy visit. She'd done her homework. I had previously sent photos of Mother's abuse, as well as other information on abuse of the elderly.

I explained that Mother's case was not an isolated incident; that determination to prevent any other family from going through what we'd endured had led to the founding of NOBLE; and a bit about NOBLE's work and goals. I expressed the desire that we make everyone aware of the problems and work together toward a solution for our nation's elderly.

"Mrs. Bush," I said, sensing that our time might be drawing to a close, "I would like to present you with a certificate of appreciation from NOBLE, to thank you for your caring and concern for our work."

"Thank you," she replied quietly, "but you really should be giving this to Randa."

"I have one to present to her in a few minutes," I whispered. "Mrs. Bush, I've also brought a packet of NOBLE's materials for you."

"Thank you," she said. "I will share them with the President."

She could not have offered me a greater gift.

Mrs. Bush then graciously turned and visited with Betty Lane and Dorothy for a few moments before saying goodbye. She had given us nearly thirty minutes of her time!

Randa concluded our visit with a private tour of the White House, the perfect end to a perfect day.

EPILOGUE: "BESSIE'S LEGACY"

Dear Mom,

I don't know where to begin! It's been such an exciting week! I actually got to meet Mrs. Bush at the White House. I wish you could have been there. But you're the reason I got to go, Mom, and I really think you were there with "your girls."

NOBLE was created for you, Mom. I know it was too late to save you from hurt and fear, and that will always be a great sadness for me. But I have to move on from that point and turn it into something good for someone else. You were always doing things for others in your sweet, gentle way. By doing our best to make people aware of the problems, and offer some helpful advice, maybe we can help save other dear souls from going through your pain. That could be a great legacy in your memory. Perhaps one day we can truly offer "Better Living for the Elderly." I hope so with all my heart.

I love you, Mom, 5/3, still and always.

XOXOX,
Your Di

11 Attention, Please, Families

No government action or agency, no advocacy foundation or individual, can insure the elderly against abuse. There are laws, agencies, and advocacy groups, and still abuse happens. It is up to each individual to accept responsibility for doing whatever he can, in whatever capacity, to end the national disgrace of elder abuse.

And that means you, and you, and you.

Each one of us could face the prospect of caring for another, or needing care ourselves at some time in our lives. Start where you are. Each family must take responsibility for ensuring the best possible care for its elder loved one, whether in the elder's own home, in the family's home, or in a long-term care facility. For some this may be an easily accepted labor of love. For others, traumatic family history might make you want to reject this responsibility. Regardless of your personal feelings, it is a responsibility. What does this responsibility mean?

It means understanding the needs of the elder. Chapter 15 offers suggestions to help assess your elder's situation and needs, to determine some of the details of everyday living, to find helpful resources, and to provide quality care at any stage of need.

It means understanding the changes and tensions associated with caregiving. Things are different. Relationships are different. Chapter 16 provides suggestions for dealing with the most common tensions.

It means a cooperative effort between the caregiver and the immediate family for the most satisfactory possible arrangements for living with the added responsibilities, concerns, demands, and, yes, rewards of contributing to the success of the loved one's elder years.

In chapters 12, 13, and 14, we challenge medical personnel, long-term care facility personnel, and government officials to consider and accept their responsibilities, and to initiate changes in their fields of expertise.

But because the primary responsibility must lie with the family, we challenge families to become informed, educated, and involved. We urge you to partner with all of these professionals, and thereby take responsibility for the overall care and protection of your elder.

Partnering with the Medical Professionals

The primary caregiver in the family should take the initiative to meet and get to know Mom's physician, who is a real person with a real life apart from the antiseptic atmosphere of the examining room. For the best cooperative care, you need to be able to discuss treatment with mutual understanding and respect. Indicate your willingness, desire, and even insistence on being included in any consideration of treatment. As one concerned physician said, "It's easier and less stressful for all to establish links before crises arise."

If you're taking Mom to the physician's office, it works well for the caregiver to go into the examining room with her, share needed information, and hear specific directions concerning her care. Then allow Mom some private time with the physician to discuss anything she might prefer to keep confidential.

If Dad is in a long-term care facility, it's more difficult to meet with the doctor; however, you could request a specific appointment at his convenience when he's scheduled to visit the facility. As the overseeing caregiver, be a mediator between the physician and your dad, facilitating the applicable suggestions in chapter 12. Help it happen.

Don't judge Mom's compatibility with the doctor too quickly; the first few visits may be awkward, so give it time. Keep open, cooperative communication with the doctor. After a number of visits, if mom's discomfort continues, it may be appropriate to request another physician. Don't be intimidated. It's best for your loved one to be comfortable with his or her physician of record. If Mom has a history of inability to accept and cooperate with her physician, you may have to use your judgment in determining what's best for her, and stand by your decision.

Partnering with Long-term Care Facilities

Chapter 15 will help you evaluate your elder's need for more care. If the indications are that a long-term care facility is the best choice for care, appendix D will help you make an informed decision.

When you place a family member in a facility, OBRA (Omnibus Budget Reconciliation Act of 1987, a federal regulation that contains major nursing home reforms, primarily in the area of residents' rights) requires the facility to schedule an assessment and care-plan meeting with family and staff members overseeing the resident's care. To be assured that all your questions and concerns are addressed, be prepared with your own list of topics and questions. As with the medical personnel, it's vital to indicate not only your willingness, but also your intent and requirement to "be there" whenever there's need.

On the day of admission, take a photo of Mom (or Dad) with the front page and the date of the daily newspaper facing the camera. This gives you a dated record showing how Mom looks on the day of admission. If the date isn't discernible in the original print, the photo can be enlarged if there's need later. Some video cameras record the date automatically. If she's able to walk, show Mom walking into the building. This gives you a visual dated record that we hope will be only a pleasant picture for your family album. But it's also a valuable tool for monitoring the progressive state of your loved one's condition. In the event of any question concerning mistreatment or abuse, there'll be a recorded "before" photo for comparison with later conditions.

Every time you visit, have a camera and a dated portion of the newspaper with you. If you notice any bruises, even if there's an apparent logical explanation, take a photo. For Dad's peace of mind, try to do it naturally, without comment, taking the photo of Dad, not just of his bruises. Keep these photos on file to review further should there be any major incident later.

Buy a notebook and, from the first day of admission, make a dated entry every visit, like a diary. This can "entertain" your elder as you visit, interviewing him about his activities, comments on TV shows he's watched or magazines and books he's read, friends he's made among the residents or staff, and any concerns he expresses. Note anything he might request you to bring on a future visit, any questions, and any complaints, minor or major. Note Dad's manner and attitude, his physical appearance and grooming, appetite, and general outlook. Listen to what Dad tells you. If he says something you find hard to believe, accept it to the extent of checking it out. Don't just automatically dismiss it. Like the photographs, the journal will give you a running account by which to monitor Dad's physical and mental states. It will also give you a tool by which to evaluate any unusual occurrences or emerging patterns.

Establish rapport with the staff. Be cooperative and helpful. Give credit where credit is due. If there are minor things you can assist with, do so, but be definite in what you need and expect. For example, "I noticed Mom's water pitcher was empty, so I filled it. She really needs to have it placed where she can reach it. Her medications make her very thirsty."

Your cooperation shows you aren't always demanding; however, your main concern is the care of your loved one. If you disagree with something the facility is doing, learn the lines of authority so you can speak with the right person to address your needs. If it has to do with actual healthcare, speak to the floor nurse in charge, usually a registered nurse (RN) or a licensed vocational nurse (LVN). If your request is not addressed, it may be necessary to go to the director of nursing or the physician. If it has to do with non-medical or general housing care, go to the appropriate department: dietitian, social services, housekeeping, activities, laundry, etc.

Again, if it's not resolved, you may need to speak with the administrator. Because of the changing shifts, it's not usually productive to make requests of the aides. It will ease your concerns and frustrations to speak to the one with the authority to initiate action or change.

By following these recommendations, you're doing your job as the family caregiver. You're visiting as often as possible, noting your observations in writing, and acting on your observations.

If you're ever confronted with major or suspicious bruising, take action at once. Ask Mom how it happened. Ask the director of nursing what medical treatment has been done or is needed. Ask whether the incident has been reported to the doctor and to the ombudsman. Ask whether a report has been made to the Licensing and Certification Department, or even to the police. Ask if it was entered on the medical records, and ask to see the records, as is your right if you hold a Durable Power of Attorney for Health Care. There are two designations, slightly different but often used interchangeably, that deal with health care and end-of-life decisions. The first, Durable Power of Attorney for Health Care, is explained in appendix C. A newer document, called an "Advance Health Care Directive" (AHCD), is more expansive. A living will is one type of advance directive, often accompanied by a power of attorney or healthcare proxy. Discuss the options with your medical care provider and your attorney before deciding which best fits your needs. (See chapter 15, paragraph A.3, and appendix C for further discussion of this invaluable tool.) With Mom's permission, if she is able to give it, you also have the right to see her medical records. Take close-up photos from several angles (using today's dated newspaper). It's recommended that you, the overseeing caregiver, call the ombudsman on your own, even if the facility has already done so. This puts you on record, reporting your concerns as the family representative.

If the trauma is obviously a major one, and the facility has not done so, call the police at once. The family must not be susceptible to the fear factor — fear of mistaken judgment, fear of retaliation. Only by reporting such incidents will we eventually gain control over them. If you don't do something about your own experience, it will be repeated with another family, and another, and perhaps even yours again. Each family must take responsibility for its own loved one, but by reporting, the dissemination of information and the resulting disciplinary action against the perpetrators will help prevent further abuses.

Partnering with Legislators and Government Officials

If you experience an incident of abuse, consider notifying your government representatives by mail or phone. Explain that you realize they aren't law enforcement, but that you simply want them to be aware of the types of things going on in violation of the regulations governing long-term care facilities. If you choose to report in person and are granted an appointment, respect the legislator's time and go prepared.

Explain that you want them to be aware of situations in long-term care facilities in their district.

Briefly explain the circumstances of the abuse.

Take your dated "before and after" photos and your journal to show that you've documented your loved one's residence at the facility.

Explain what the facility has or has not done to resolve the situation.

Explain that you will keep the legislator informed of the progress of the situation.

Ask if the legislator has established a task force for elder issues.

In chapter 14 we urge government representatives to inform themselves on the vital issue of elder abuse and to take responsibility for addressing the problem. We've recommended and outlined the establishment of task forces, which are committees on any designated subject, for keeping legislators informed on various issues, and providing a vehicle for needed change.

Any legislator can sponsor a task force for elder issues, and we ask all legislators to consider establishing such committees in their areas for the purpose of becoming informed, networking information, and creating united, coordinated legislative action to correct the problems of elder abuse.

Chairing such a task force is something you or another member of your family might consider offering to do for your legislator. I served as chairman of my state legislator's task force, the composition of which is outlined in appendix H. This is offered as an example if your legislator does not yet sponsor such a task force.

Closure After Abuse

Once you've experienced an incident of abuse in a long-term care facility, after you notify the ombudsman and/or the police as well as a local advocacy group (if you know of such a group), there'll be a time of waiting while those agencies make their investigations. In California, the facility must notify the Department of Health Services, Licensing and Certification. They must also notify the ombudsman or the local police department. Your local ombudsman can inform you of the required reporting procedures for your state, and advise you how to keep informed of the status of the investigation.

The result could be a finding anywhere in a broad range, from no accountability to full accountability with resulting disciplinary action. If the finding is acceptable to you, so be it. If, however, you do not agree with the finding, you may take further action as described in the written notification from the Licensing and Certification Department. In California you may request a hearing to cite your disagreement with the finding and to appeal the decision. Be prepared to take all your documentation, photos, journal, and any new facts you may be aware of. Request that Licensing reopen and reinvestigate the incident. (See appendix G for help in preparing for this meeting.) If the new finding is still unacceptable, you have the recourse of requesting an investigation by the state-level office overseeing this department. Of course, at any time in the process you have the option of seeking legal advice and filing civil action against a facility or an individual.

You and your family must decide on a goal that will provide personal closure for you. You truly can't put this behind you and move on until you define what will end it for you. Perhaps you'll consider one of the investigative findings appropriate and acceptable. If that's not the case, you need to determine that you've done everything that you yourself can do. For some, this means active advocacy work. For some, it means support groups. For some, it means telling your story to the media. For some, it means getting active politically. For some, it means volunteering. For some, it can be as simple as handholding for another family suffering this situation.

Even when you accept that you've done everything possible and are able to close the doors on this chapter, you'll still experience moments of remembrance. Some may be bitter. You have to learn to live with those moments and choose to close the door again.

You do what you can, and what you need to, and then you decide when you have closure.

Attention, please, families.

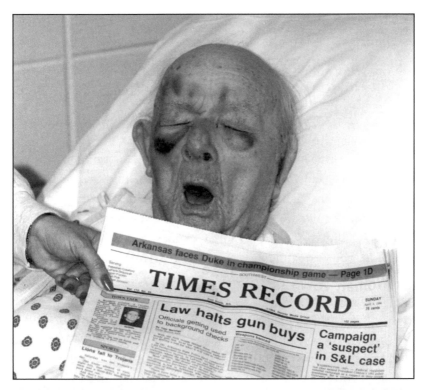

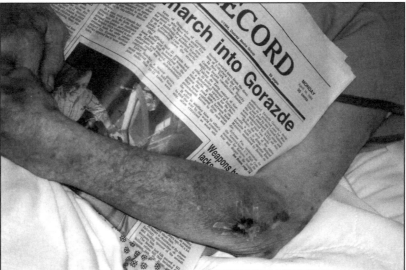

Newspaper documents the date of abuse

12 ATTENTION PLEASE, PHYSICIANS AND MEDICAL PERSONNEL

Many of us grew up with a "God fixation" about physicians and medical personnel. In doctors' offices, hospitals, and testing labs, hushed voices, antiseptic odors, and starched uniforms inspired respectful awe tinged with fear. We crowned our medical heroes with halos of infallibility, never presuming to question or challenge any recommendation or treatment.

The age of easy lawsuits has changed all that. On the positive side, we have protection and recourse for improper or truly inadequate treatment. On the negative side, however, frivolous lawsuits have driven up the cost of insurance protection, further raising costs of treatment, and elevating frustration on both sides of the examination room. We place our heroes on pedestals, then contribute to nudging them off.

Humanizing our medical professionals has advantages. To assure the best overall healthcare program for any patient (in this case, the care of our elders), the medical professional, the elder and his or her family, and the personnel of long-term care facilities need to learn to work cooperatively.

Many of the suggestions that follow are simply common sense and good human relations in any situation, but are sometimes overlooked in our harried, fast-paced lifestyle. We respectfully ask that the physicians and other medical personnel who read these words accept them in the spirit in which they are offered. We also ask family members and other non-medical personnel to consider these suggestions reciprocally. Both the positive and the negative examples are taken from the many cases I have worked with. No finger-pointing is intended; there is only the hope for better relations all around, win-win situations, and results.

All Medical Personnel, Please

Introduce yourself distinctly, by title, on your first contact. If the patient's mental awareness necessitates it, repeat on successive visits.

As a matter of respect, use patients' last names and titles (Mr., Mrs., Miss, Dr., Rev., etc.). Don't use first names unless specifically requested to, or familiar non-names (dear, honey), which can be patronizing. Elders deserve the dignity too often stripped from them when they become dependent on assisted living arrangements. They have contributed to society as parents, teachers, scientists, doctors, attorneys, clergy, musicians, writers, artists, businesspersons, lawmakers, merchants, technicians, and myriad other careers.

See your patients as real human beings, not as case files. Take the time to learn about their personal histories as well as their medical histories.

Make yourself aware of the circumstances surrounding the elders in your care, whether you attend them in their own or a caregiver's home, in an office or lab setting, in a long-term care facility, or in the hospital.

Consider that, like children, many of these elders are frightened because they are no longer in control. They don't like or understand the changes in their lives. Win their trust and respect by treating them with dignity and respect. If you are considerate, and the patient is cognizant of what's going on, he or she will respond in kind. If you're abrupt and impersonal, a negative reaction is likely. In my mother's case, facility personnel referred to her several times as "combative," as if that excused the fact that someone beat her twice in one night while she was restrained, unable to protect herself. As a matter of record, the psychiatrist who had earlier been called in to examine her cited her graciousness throughout the interview, and her expressed regret that she couldn't offer him a cup of tea. She was responding in kind to the manner in which he treated her.

By reason of your objectivity you may be able to help elders and their families better understand a situation in a care facility, and help facility personnel better understand the care of residents. Better understanding on all sides results in more satisfactory care and more satisfied residents and families.

While some personal family physicians visit facility residents, if your services are referred through the facility, you need to be the resident's physician, not the facility's physician. By virtue of your Hippocratic oath, your first concern must be for your patient.

Physicians need to be direct with the facility; if the facility isn't doing the job, you have the power and the responsibility to exert influence. The physician should be "the boss" over the resident's care. Treatment should be for the good of the resident, not the convenience of the facility.

Physicians need to be direct with the resident's family. If they aren't doing their job in support of their elder, you have the influence to make recommendations that might result in a better atmosphere. Whenever possible, maintain open communication with the family.

In the case of a long-term care facility resident who doesn't have any family, you may be the only outside influence in that person's life. Because of the ages of this particular generation of residents, and their ingrained regard for your profession, you have the power to greatly enhance their lives with encouraging, understanding support. Take the time to acquaint yourself with residents as much as they are able to respond. Don't just take cold data from a case file.

There's an inside joke about doctors being the worst patients. Consider what it might be like if you were in the resident's bed. We ask caregivers to imagine infirmities like weakened eyesight and hearing, arthritic joints, immobility, painful medical conditions, and loss of dignity. We also ask medical personnel to take the time to consider these limitations. Just as we drill medical teams for emergency situations, it might be worth a graphic role-playing exercise in a training seminar to demonstrate these limitations, using medical personnel as the infirm elders.

If more than one physician treats a resident, check past records, consider the effects, interactions, and reactions of multiple medications, and the possible adverse results. There have been many cases of drug use for behavior control and restraint, resulting in inactive, incoherent, nonfunctioning patients. In some fortunate cases, discontinuing excessive medication has resulted in the resident reverting to normal functioning behavior.

Regarding physical abuse, physicians, remember: you are mandated reporters. Don't be hasty to dismiss bruising as natural for older skin, the result of bumps and falls. The facility physician dismissed the bruising on the top of my mother's head as likely resulting from a fall; the handprint on her face as having possibly been caused when someone picked her up! This could only have happened had she had fallen directly onto the top of her head and been picked up by her face! Learn the signs of covert abuse. Consider the humanity of the resident and let your righteous indignation determine your advocacy. Look for repeat bruising. Ask members of the staff, not just the management, what the climate is in the facilities you visit. Many nurses and aides have reported being afraid to blow the whistle for fear of losing their jobs; some who've reported abuse situations have been fired. Be an advocate for those who are trying to do their jobs well and compassionately.

If the physician is doing the job properly, he or she will already be doing these things. We don't intend to insult your intelligence with these commonsense suggestions. There are, however, far too many instances of residents being simply warehoused and receiving production-line treatment and medication, resulting in avoidable dire consequences.

Don't be defensive if a family elects to choose another physician. It may be the comfort or compatibility level of the resident or the family with the physician that makes a switch advisable. By the same token, don't hesitate to recommend another physician if you feel that a resident's personality, or that of the family, doesn't mesh with your own.

Physicians, you determine how you are respected at the facilities. If you overlook infractions and carelessness in others, or justify it in your own modus operandi, your integrity is at stake. So is that of the facility, not only with residents, families, and the general public, but with those individuals within the system who strive to operate at their professional best. When you afford dignity to staff members and residents, your attitude and demeanor help set the tone for optimum conditions for all.

In public presentations on the prevalence of abuse in long-term care facilities, I strive to be fair. I always make the point that there are good facilities, there are good physicians, and there are good nurses, CNAs, and facility staffs. If we're all doing our jobs as we should, why is there any need for defensiveness? How much abuse is allowable? How much neglect is tolerable? Can any abuse of fragile elders be acceptable?

One can be taught the science of medicine, but one must also learn the art of medicine. We don't expect you to be gods, but we do ask you to be "the physician." Think about why you became a physician. The medical profession differs from any other because of its power of life or death, and therefore carries responsibilities like no other profession.

Attention, please, physicians and medical personnel.

> *I swear…*
> *that I will carry out,*
> *according to my ability and judgment,*
> *this oath…I will use treatment to help the sick*
> *according to my ability and judgment,*
> *but never with a view to injury and wrongdoing.*
> *I will keep pure and holy both my life and my art.*
> *In whatsoever houses I enter, I will enter to help the sick,*
> *and I will abstain from all intentional wrong-doing and harm.*
> *…Now if I carry out this oath, and break it not,*
> *may I gain forever reputation among all men*
> *for my life and for my art;*
> *but if I transgress it and forswear myself,*
> *may the opposite befall me.*
>
> The Physician's Oath
> Hippocrates
> 460–337 BC

13 ATTENTION PLEASE, ADMINISTRATORS AND CORPORATE MANAGEMENT

Attention, please, Mr. CEO, Ms. President of Long-term Care, Mrs. Administrator. If you found yourself suddenly in the position of placing your loved one — Mom, Dad, Grandma — into a facility within two days, expecting dignified, quality care without exception, could you find it?

Of course! thinks Mr. CEO. One of our corporation's facilities. They're the finest in the industry.

Of course! thinks Ms. President of Long-term Care. But wait — there is that lawsuit pending.

Of course! thinks Mrs. Administrator. But wait — must I now worry about that new person I just hired?

Is there a place good enough for your mom, Mr. CEO? Do you really know your facilities?

Is there a place good enough for your dad, Ms. President? How many of your facilities received citations during their most recent inspections?

Is there a place good enough for your grandma, Mrs. Administrator? Are you careful enough about who works in your facility?

Families are apprehensive when they place a loved one in a facility. It's new to them. They're concerned. They've seen the disturbing investigative programs on TV. They've read the newspapers' graphic accounts of elder abuse. Still, they have to place Mother by Monday morning. They have to trust. They want to trust. Sometimes, they can trust.

There are well-run facilities that provide dignified, quality care. It begins with the administrator, who sets the tone for the entire operation.

She hires a highly qualified staff that meets her high standards. She senses their work ethic and their regard for the elderly. She oversees training, and interjects her personal expectations of excellence. Hers is a facility to be recognized, recommended, and emulated.

The facility where I moved my mother after her abuse exemplified these practices. (In fact, to be entirely fair, my sister and I had, in the past, sent letters of commendation to the facility where the abuse later took place, citing specific instances of what we felt had been exemplary treatment.) From the first visit with the director of admissions, the positive atmosphere of the new facility was apparent in the gentleness with which they handled Mother, their providing the special bed, and the continuous nurturing by all the staff to rebuild her sense of security.

It can be done!

Just as the administrator sets the tone for the facility, the CEO sets the tone for the corporation. Because this is a business specifically to care for our elderly, the responsibility and accountability for dignified, quality care must begin and end with the CEO. Throughout the entire organization, from the executive officers to the facility staff, the CEO must determine, delegate, and demand compliance with expectations.

We need excellent corporations and facilities in business. We certainly want them to make a profit. As families and advocates, we surely want to work with the industry to assure this dignified, quality care. We appreciate those who do the job well. But you and I know, Mr. CEO, Ms. President of Long-term Care, Mrs. Administrator, that there are those who don't do the job well. There is neglect and there is abuse — to the point of death-inducing conditions — even in facilities considered first-rate. How can we tolerate this? When will we acknowledge the problem and determine to fix it? Let's do it now. It's in everyone's best interests: we're in a partnership — it's our responsibility.

The first step in solving any problem is to recognize and accept that there is a problem. Until we acknowledge a problem, we can't fix it. Why can some facilities and corporations provide this care? Why can't they all? What will it take to accomplish dignified, quality care?

Corporation management personnel need to have information. How far up the chain and in what detail are reports of problems discussed? Mr. CEO, do you know? Anywhere along the chain of reporting, an employee protecting his job may fail to report an incident, make light of an incident, or make excuses for it. Aides tending to my mother the night of her abuse saw, but assumed her condition had been reported. The CNA in charge of her room claimed she had not abused the resident, in fact purposely avoided her due to verbal and physical abuse of the staff (by an eighty-five pound, ninety-one-year-old strapped into bed).

There was no question in my mind that Mother had been beaten. I called the police, who came within the hour and investigated the case as "assault and battery." Three days later, the physician said the bruises could have been caused by a fall and by attendants picking her up. Licensing and Certification did not investigate for nearly a month, though clear regulations dictate that suspected abuse must be investigated within twenty-four hours. Where did the system break down? There are many ways to circumvent accountability. Are we going to accept that? Don't you want to fix the areas causing the industry a bad reputation, costing the industry in insurance, fines, and defense fees, costing family trauma and sometimes even lives? These could be your own parents!

CEOs and presidents, you need to be in dialogue with the ombudsman's office in each area where you have a facility. You need to be open to dialogue with families and advocates of residents. We urge you to engage in dialogue with the legislators in your state, speaking to their task forces about what it will take to solve the problem of providing the kind of care you want your parent to receive. Are you willing to consider an independent, objective troubleshooter, who reports directly to you, unbiased by close involvement with a facility?

Corporations, as providers of long-term care, and CEOs, as the final authority, have a responsibility to ensure that the physicians practicing in the facility are of the same high quality they'd hire to look after their own moms. You set the standard and pass it down. Establish that overlooking neglect and abuse will not be tolerated. Establish that Medicare/Medicaid abuse (fraud) will not be tolerated. You know it happens. We know it happens. In northern California, indictments were brought against a physician specializing in geriatric medicine, and against the owner of a skilled nursing facility, totaling $4 million in false Medicare billings. In that district alone, fraud drains at least $1 billion a year out of the healthcare industry (reported in *The Sacramento Bee,* April 20, 1994). Nor is the problem confined to any one district or state. Is it any wonder that the long-term care industry must contend with a bad reputation?

We ask administrators to live up to the impression given by the admissions office interviewing to accept new residents. Continuing a dialogue with families and advocates who only want dignified quality care for elders brings us all into the partnership of responsibility. We've challenged families to inform themselves, to cooperate, to be responsible for their part in supporting their elder residents. We challenge administrators in kind.

We know there is the human element, involving so many people of differing histories and temperaments and care requirements, from both the resident's and the caregiver's side of the picture. We know there can be frustration and aggravation on both sides of the bed rail. But please don't label a family as troublemakers when they're simply concerned about Grandma's welfare. Families do get frustrated when Grandma's dinner tray is plunked down, out of her reach, grabbed up later when she still hasn't had a chance to eat, and her chart notes that she ate 80% of her meal. Why, then, has she lost twenty pounds in two months? What about *your* grandma?

Families do get frustrated when Dad's chair is wheeled down the hall so fast that he cries out that his feet can't keep up and that they hurt. What about *your* dad? Families do get frustrated when Mother is held over the toilet by two male aides, or left, uncovered, on her bed after returning from a shower. What about *your* mother? What about you, Mrs. Administrator? Can you truly defend these practices as acceptable and necessary?

Accept the responsibility when your staff doesn't do the job. When a mistake is made, admit it, correct it, and go forward. The needed correction might entail training; it might be a reprimand; or it might be immediate dismissal.

We need to offer CNAs dignity and respect on the job. Theirs is the hands-on daily grind of caregiving. Without them the nursing-home industry would fail completely. Let's investigate them fully before hiring, fingerprint them for the corporation's assurance and the resident's protection, train them properly for the job, pay them well, and offer incentives and bonuses such as a period of paid free time after a specified period of good service for jobs well done. With loyal staff feeling appreciated, absenteeism will be reduced, and you won't have to use temporary registry personnel so often. Use a suggestion box, available to staff, residents, and families, for suggestions for improved services, and an appreciation box for recognition of work well done.

Because of the inevitable occasion of the death of a resident, and the typical three-shift scheduling of staff, it's probable that one or more of the resident's caregivers won't be on the premises till the next shift change. Don't surprise these employees with a new resident already settled in the room. Establish some provision in the schedule at shift change to allow staff to acknowledge the loss before plunging into the routine of the new shift.

Make it easier for staff to report abuse without fear of losing their jobs. You are all mandated reporters. Families should be free to report abuse without fear of retaliation. Covering it up to protect the facility's "reputation" only leads to a poorer reputation. Instead, why don't we fix what's wrong so we can be proud of what's right?

Couldn't we all work together to respect the dignity of the residents and the staffs in our long-term care facilities? Some of the problems currently experienced wouldn't arise because they'd already be taken care of. Isn't it worth it?

Consider this articulate poem by an unidentified writer, found in one woman's bedside stand after she died in a nursing home.

Look Closer — See Me

What do you see, nurses, what do you see?
Are you thinking when you are looking at me —
A crabby old woman, not very wise,
Uncertain of habit, with faraway eyes.
Who dribbles her food and makes no reply
When you say in a loud voice, "I do wish you'd try."
Who seems not to notice the things that you do,
And forever is losing a stocking or shoe.
Who unresisting or not, lets you do as you will,
With bathing and feeding, the long day to fill.
Is that what you are thinking; is that what you see?
Then open your eyes, nurse, YOU'RE NOT LOOKING AT ME!
I'll tell you who I am, as I sit here so still,
As I use at your bidding, as I eat at your will,
I'm a small child of ten with a father and mother,
Brother and sisters, who love one another,
A young girl of sixteen with wings on her feet,
Dreaming that soon now a lover she'll meet;
A bride soon at twenty — my heart gives a leap,
Remembering the vows that I promise to keep;
At twenty-five now I have young of my own;
Who need me to build a secure, happy home.
 A woman at thirty, my young now grow fast;
Bound to each other with ties that should last.
At forty, my young sons have grown and have gone,
But my man's beside me to see I don't mourn.
At fifty once more babies play 'round my knee,
Again we know children, my loved one and me.
Dark days are upon me, my husband is dead,
I look at the future, I shudder with dread,
For my young are still rearing young of their own,
And I think of the years and the love that I've known.

I'm an old woman now and nature is cruel —
'Tis her jest to make old age look like a fool.
The body it crumbles, grace and vigor depart,
There is now a stone where I once had a heart.
But inside this old carcass a young girl still dwells.
And now and again my battered heart swells,
I remember the joys, I remember the pain,
And I'm loving and living life over again.
I think of the years all too few — gone too fast;
And accept the stark fact that nothing can last.
So open your eyes, nurses, open and see,
Not a crabby old woman — look closer — SEE ME.

~:~

We challenge every corporation in the industry to be the trendsetter. Mr. CEO, will you publicly state that there's a better way? Will you publicly state that you're going to set the pace and turn this industry around? Will you publicly state that you'll initiate new criteria, new standards, new education, new practices, and new open communication? Will you publicly offer to share with other corporations and the public what's working, what's making a difference? You would reap the benefits of better care, better public relations, better employee relations, fewer fines, lower defense fees, lower insurance rates — but more than that, the knowledge that you could, with full assurance, face any family member of any resident, and even your own mother.

Let's prove that it can be done and done well. Will you be the first?

Question: "Mr. CEO, what would you have done had this been your mother?"

Answer (from the CEO of the corporation in whose facility my mother was beaten): "Mrs. Sandell, I'd probably have done exactly what you're doing."

And that's the bottom line.

Attention, please, administrators and corporate management.

Government is a trust, and the officers of the government are trustees; and both the trust and the trustees are created for the benefit of the people.

— Henry Clay, 1829

It is not enough for a great nation merely to have added new years to life— our objective must also be to add new life to those years.

— John F. Kennedy, 1963

14 ATTENTION, PLEASE, LEGISLATORS AND GOVERNMENT OFFICIALS

Attention, please, legislators and government officials — Ms. Mayor, Mr. City Councilman, Ms. County Supervisor, Mr. Assemblyman, Ms. Representative, Mr. Senator, Ms. Governor, Mr. President — Mr./Ms. Any Official.

We do have laws about abuse of the elderly. But we still have a big problem, a silent problem, a city, county, and state problem adding up to a national disgrace. We don't want to talk about it or read about it. Does that mean we don't want to do anything about it? It would seem so. It's hard to draw any other conclusion.

Legislators, we know you aren't law enforcement, and we don't expect you to be. But do you know the extent of the problem? Do you know what kind of elder abuse is occurring in the long-term care facilities in your city? Do you know there's a way to find out? Do you know where you would place your mother if she suddenly needed to be in a skilled nursing facility?

Do you know the extent of elder abuse in your district or state? Do you know what agencies regulate and oversee the facilities in your state? Do you know the procedures of the agencies regulating long-term care? What will you do when your dad can't be cared for at home? Do you know how to find the best facility?

Do you know what percentage of the population of your state is in long-term care facilities? Do you know the incidence of abuse? Do you know how often certain facilities appear on the investigation reports? Where will your older sister be placed if no one in the family can care for her? What about you? Any chance you might become a resident of a long-term care facility? Do you know what to expect there?

We recommend that all government officials visit the long-term care facilities in their own districts, to observe firsthand their constituents' care and learn the answers to these questions.

Although some encouraging steps have been taken, elders are still being beaten, intimidated, over-medicated, left unclothed while waiting for their showers, left in their own urine and feces, ignored, and neglected. When are we going to get shocked enough or angry enough to do something definitive about it? Perhaps only when it happens to someone we personally love?

Talking to everyone who would listen has been a revealing odyssey. The congressman of my district heard my story and invited me to share it with his Senior Citizen Task Force. When he later went to Washington as United States Senator, I encouraged his successor to establish his own task force to keep informed on issues of the elderly. In turn he asked me to chair the committee. Details on establishing a task force are included in appendix H.

In the following months, I was granted appointments with congressmen, senators, county supervisors, assemblymen, and various regulatory officials at local and federal levels. Because I went fully prepared and was considerate of their time, I was always received with respect, concern, and consideration.

We appeal to you elected officials. You were chosen by a majority of the voters. You have a responsibility to your entire constituency, even those confined in long-term care facilities. You have an opportunity to be a crusader for real improvement in the lives of the elderly — and won't we all be there someday?

You hold the key to the door to legislation that can make a difference. Please open that door. There are advocacies for birds, fish, whales, trees, wetlands, wilderness lands, and so on. In a nation that can send a man to the moon, why must our frail elderly fear for their dignity, their safety, and even their lives? Listen to constituents who ask to share their stories. We understand your busyness, but aren't your constituents' concerns your business? Grant just fifteen minutes. It can make a difference. Listen with an ear to informing yourself. Use the following suggestions to increase your knowledge and awareness, and then devote time to writing legislation to resolve these issues.

Don't assume the cases you hear about are isolated. For every one who attempts to see you, many more are experiencing similar problems but don't know where to turn to ask for help.

Don't assume that the media give the whole picture. There is excellent coverage, and there is sensational coverage. Sensational coverage makes the headlines for a day, but is quickly forgotten. Excellent coverage attempts to provide correct information and awareness, but even that doesn't result in correcting the problems unless those with interest, ability, and authority choose to act. Seek out more information. Subscribe to one of the advocate organization newsletters. Use a clipping service, or create a volunteer one. Meet the ombudsman in your area and ask what, specifically, would help solve the problem. Establish a task force to gather information and make recommendations. Initiate a dialogue with representatives in other areas, perhaps encouraging a network of task forces for the purpose of coordinating information and possible legislation. With concerted, coordinated effort, innovative pilot programs might spotlight your district, your county, and your state as the front-runner in the field of superlative eldercare.

What about your campaign contributions? Do you really know from whom you're accepting contributions? The long-term care industry invests heavily in electing legislators. Contributions are given through individuals' names, giving no indication of association with the industry. When corporation names are given, they don't always reveal the field of industry they represent. Why is the industry interested in supporting a candidacy? What do they expect in return? Will it have an impact on your decision making? How do you feel about that? How might you feel if your parent had been severely beaten in a facility owned by a corporation that had contributed to your campaign?

What will it take to make a difference? It seems a harsh indictment, but we believe the only way things will change for the better will be to make it too costly for the industry not to improve care. Some regulations are in place, but if they're not enforced there is no incentive. Complaints may be processed, and facilities investigated and cited without fines. But fines are often waived because of various options open to the industry. *The CANHR ADVOCATE* (the newsletter of the California Advocates for Nursing Home Reform, March 1996, Volume VI, No. 4, San Francisco, CA) reports:

> "For the past ten years, nursing home advocates and consumers have witnessed the dilution of California's citation and fine system as it relates to nursing homes. Originally established to provide an enforcement incentive for poor performing facilities to comply with the laws, the system has gradually eroded to the point that fewer citations and fines are issued each year and few monetary penalties are collected...."

The industry sometimes charges that the advocacy groups are biased against it. But when we compare the viewpoint of industry, which, understandably, must be operated for profit, with that of advocacy groups, many of which are staffed by volunteers working solely for quality care, where is the basis for a charge of bias? In that we simply want better care for our elderly, yes, perhaps we are biased. We want industry to do the job successfully and profitably. We need successful well-run facilities, and we'll need more in the future as our aging population swells with the influx of the Boomer generation. Let's cooperate to get the job done and still provide dignified, quality care. Let's establish what needs to be done, determine what it will cost, and then find ways of providing funds to accomplish the task.

Many factors have excessively driven up the costs of providing quality care. We need to definitively end the Medicare-Medicaid fraud situation, make those operators accountable, and initiate checks and balances that are not now in place. Freeing up monies misused through fraud and its defense could then provide more funds for proper daily care allotments.

Fingerprinting. California Senate Bill 945 (1998) requires fingerprinting of designated personnel: certified nurse assistants (CNAs), home health aides (HHAs), students enrolling in CNA/HHA training programs, and home health agency owners and administrators in virtually all facilities — skilled nursing, intermediate care, intermediate care for the developmentally disabled, home health agencies, nurse assistant and home health training programs, accredited nursing schools, general acute care hospitals, and hospices.

Notification procedures. Current regulation in California requires skilled long-term care facilities to report suspected abuse to the Department of Health Services, Licensing and Certification, and to notify either the ombudsman program or the local police department. That regulation should, in our opinion, require the immediate notification of both the ombudsman program and the local police department.

Designations. "Unusual occurrence." Unless the "unusual occurrence" designation is clearly defined, it removes the urgency from necessity to investigate immediately because it depends on the description of the incident. According to California regulations, "unusual occurrences" must be identified and reported within twenty-four hours to the Licensing and Certification Department, where they are assigned a priority based on description of the incident. Patient abuse must be investigated within twenty-four hours, but the reporting and handling of an incident depends on the integrity of all personnel involved. In my mother's case, LCD did not investigate for nearly a month. We recommend the designation "unusual occurrence" be eliminated entirely, in favor of a more definitive term, or amended by a mandatory further clarification of the nature of the "unusual occurrence."

Legislators and government officials, what can you do?

There are many possible recommendations. We suggest that legislators nationwide adopt measures similar to California SB 679, The Elder Abuse and Dependent Adult Civil Protection Act, previously referenced in chapter 7, and California SB 945. Other protective measures are in effect in California and in other states. The most important consideration, however, would be interstate and national dialogue, standardization of regulations throughout the nation, effective enforcement, and education of the public — in a clear, simple, standardized format — of the protective laws in effect. A publication for this purpose would be of the greatest community service.

Issue informed statements to the media, telling them that, like child abuse and spousal abuse, elder abuse cannot and will not be tolerated. Why do we even have to say that? When the long-term care industry understands that every area of government will take a proactive stand to protect our elder citizens, backed by legislation and enforcement, perhaps it will be brought to the "bargaining table" to solve these problems cooperatively, creatively, and productively without a defensive need to sweep things under the table. Let's work together to determine what it will take financially — without excuses, without waste, without fraud, without abuse — to provide dignified quality care for our elders, and then determine how to make it happen.

What can one person in government do? What is your responsibility? Think about why you became a legislator. Predetermine to do the right thing. Respond accordingly.

Attention, please, legislators and government officials.

15 EVALUATING YOUR ELDER'S CARE

No matter what you read or hear about the quality of life of America's senior population, it's difficult to know what to expect or plan for until you face a situation that affects you personally. Then you're emotionally involved and vulnerable.

The following five-step plan will help you assess your situation. It deliberately starts before placing a loved one in long-term care, but it can be adapted to situations arising both before and after placement. The key is creative problem solving. This plan is a "thought-starter" to help you walk through various circumstances you might be facing.

NOBLE Five-step Plan for Evaluating And Improving Eldercare

You've begun to realize that your parent or other loved one needs more care. Whether he or she has been living independently and needs more assistance to continue, or has been living with you and is growing more dependent, roles are changing. The following five steps will provide focus for evaluating the situation:

A. Assessing the Situation

1. What is the reality?

As your parent ages, there may be changes in personality that affect your relationship. Accept this new reality; don't take things personally. Try to seek positive and constructive solutions. Some personality changes respond well to medication and should be discussed with your physician. In some cases, judicious use of medications can restore a sense of well-being and normalcy, extending the period of productivity and self-sufficiency in an elder's life. This is in no way a blanket endorsement of medication for mood adjustment — a practice commonly overused to the point of abuse.

This can be one of the most frustrating seasons for the caregiver or decision maker. The frustration is understandable. It isn't wrong, but simply a negative factor to be faced and resolved. Try to maintain calm. Irritation is contagious; it makes the elder more irrational and fearful. Use the suggestions in this plan to formulate your own plan for dealing specifically with your situation.

2. What's my role?

Some, not all, elderly lose their ability to make decisions, and may regress to childhood — a time when all their needs were met by others. You may begin to feel like the parent to your parent one day, only to find your parent back in control the next. Whenever possible, encourage your parent to make his or her own decisions, but be prepared to step in tactfully when necessary. Consider options ahead of time so you're prepared to smooth over difficult situations. Getting caught off guard allows frustrations and irritations to build.

Sometimes it's prudent to make "deals" or tradeoffs to allow the parent to retain dignity, with the protections of safeguards established by the caregiver. For example: If Mom can no longer safely prepare meals at the stove, perhaps she can wash the vegetables for storage, help plan menus, make shopping lists, clip coupons, or fold grocery bags. If Dad can no longer manage the checkbook or the banking, perhaps an offer to help "translate that confusing bank statement form" would allow him to retain his dignity. Or invite him to read the ad pages for the best sales on something you need. If personal grooming becomes a problem, you might "deal" for an outing: "When you're finished with your bath, we'll go to the store (or the post office, the bank, or the ice-cream parlor, or stroll through the park around the corner)." The break will be good for both of you.

Sometimes the issue will be of greater importance. Dad may not be able to drive safely anymore. You can't protect his dignity at the expense of someone else's life; you can, however, appeal to his sense of dignity at facing and making a right choice: "Dad, we love you. We don't want to chance losing you. And we know you don't want to be responsible for hurting someone else." Mom may not be reliable to baby-sit anymore. You can't endanger her or your children for fear of hurting her feelings: "Mom, our friend, Nancy, is going to come play with the kids while we're out to dinner. I'll bet she'd like to learn some of your old children's songs to teach other kids she stays with." Dad may forget to take his medicine properly. Mom may imagine a threat to her safety — seeing people or things that aren't there. Issues of this nature must be resolved firmly, but as gently and tactfully as possible.

3. Can I really handle this? What if I need help?

Only you can decide how much you're willing and able to handle. If there are other members of the elder's family, call a meeting to discuss options. Perhaps another relative would share some of the responsibility, take Mom or Dad for a month, a week, a day, or even just an outing. Or "sit" at your house while you get out for a lunch or dinner, shopping or a movie. Or share the expense of hiring a companion while you get away for a weekend. There are families in which this cooperative effort works well; there are also families who won't even consider it, who won't offer a minute or a dime to help.

Remember that some family members simply can't face certain types of deterioration in a parent's condition, and can't force themselves even to relieve the caregiver. Seeing her dad in a helpless condition so emotionally wounded one daughter that she could spend only minutes at his bedside, and put off visits for weeks. In this case the daughter-in-law became the caregiver, able to deal with the deterioration more objectively.

If you're carrying the responsibility for the care without help from others, clarify your own responsibility and commitment. If you've been designated as having the Durable Power of Attorney for Health Care (see appendix C), you needn't share the decision making with those who don't share the physical, mental, or financial burdens. If, however, a financial estate is involved, family members who are unwilling to share the responsibilities may sometimes still try to influence or control essential decisions, or challenge your right to do so. An objective arbiter — a physician, a minister, or even an attorney — might be worthwhile and necessary to resolve differences. A Durable Power of Attorney for Health Care is strongly recommended, but requires early planning.

Within your immediate family, try to make the care of your elder a family undertaking if possible, sharing the work and responsibility as well as the fun, the sense of "family," and the rewards of knowing, loving, and serving your beloved elder. There will be painful memories as well as good, but there can be a great heritage of family history and memories when it's truly a cooperative family effort. When there are tense times, allow all family members to "own" their own feelings and reactions, even negative ones, with some ground rules regarding expression of those feelings.

Outside resources are available, both for home care and for placing elders in care facilities. These vary widely from city to city and area to area, so help yourself by learning what your area offers in the way of support and assistance (see section C below).

4. Am I doing the right thing?

Regardless of how you elect to handle your situation, there will be people who think you should have done it differently. You must think through your emotions, abilities, resources, motives, strengths, and weaknesses honestly. Make the decision first in your own mind, and then with the significant others whose lives will be directly affected. Then smile graciously with no comment to those who disagree with your decision. All these subjects are further discussed in chapter 16.

B. Caring for the Caregiver

You're tired. You're not sure how much more you can take. You want to do the right thing, but it gets harder and harder. Mom pouts, or Dad keeps repeating those stories of the old days. You're beginning to have doubts.

1. Will anyone understand?

Anyone who deals with eldercare, whether in the home or in an institutional setting, will understand and believe what you've been going through. Fortunately, much more media attention is being given to the problems of eldercare, and there's more awareness of the needs of the caregiver as well as the needs and problems of the elder. An informed primary-care physician is likely to be aware of the need for respite care, and to know some of the resources available locally.

2. Who can help? Whom can I trust?

Many cities have senior citizen centers that provide various types of diversionary help: adult classes, entertainment, therapeutic programs, even day-trips for more active adults, and daycare supervision with activities for less active seniors. There may also be adult day healthcare centers that provide a wider range of services, including physical therapy, speech therapy, and other services for special needs. Many senior citizen centers can provide lists of available resources, such as paid companions or even volunteers who can provide you a few hours of freedom to pursue your own interests. Some churches now offer this type of daycare service to the community, and hospitals often have referrals for resources in the area. For your own reassurance, check into the sponsorship of these types of programs, just as you would for one of your children.

The diversions of such programs, for both the elder and the caregiver, are well worth the time and effort to make use of them. Don't be discouraged by Dad's hesitations or Mom's complaints; the attention of and interaction with other people usually bring around your reluctant senior, and you need the refreshment of time for yourself.

3. I need help right now. Who can help?

One of the best therapies for the caregiver is a good friend whom you can call when you need a break and a different perspective. This must be someone who understands your position and won't scold you for your decision to care for your elder or for your temporary weakness or frustration. It also needs to be a person who won't be turned off by your need for this outlet and won't discuss it with others. This is no place for an "I told you so." If necessary, agree to a few minutes to let off steam, but then change the subject and talk about some interest you and your friend have in common — a book, a hobby, what's for dinner — anything to defuse high emotion brought on by your situation. Don't let it become a gripe session; the idea is to get your mind off it and give you a break from it.

If you're hesitant to burden a friend, find a support group. If you can't find a support group, start one yourself. See appendix I for suggestions. Don't shy away from this vital source of encouragement — it can save your life.

4. Am I doing the right thing?

Anything you can do to increase the possibility of success is the right thing. Using community resources can give you just the break necessary to continue facing the situation at home. Don't be ashamed or afraid to reach out for help from the outside.

C. Learning the Resources

The feeling of being all alone in your situation can be your worst enemy. Educate yourself about all possible sources of help, whether continuing to care for your elder at home or assessing the possibility of long-term facility care. Be a detective and a student. The following suggestions can get you started, but you may discover other resources. Network with everyone you can think of. Let them know your situation. You'll be surprised at the number of people who have similar situations and can offer suggestions and ideas.

Information Resources: Family Physician ⁓ Hospital Geriatric Departments ⁓ Area Agency on Aging (terminology for these departments varies) ⁓ Ombudsman Program ⁓ Social Services Agency ⁓ Department of Health Services ⁓ Adult Protective Services.

Disease-related Associations: Alzheimer's :~ Parkinson's :~ Multiple Sclerosis :~ Cancer :~ Heart :~ Others.

Support Systems: Caregiver support groups and self-help groups :~ Internet listings :~ Grassroots advocacy groups :~ Ask hospitals, newspapers, churches, colleges :~ Ask Senior Citizen Centers :~ Ask disease related associations :~ Consider starting a support group (see appendix I) :~ Respite Care :~ Some hospitals and nursing homes maintain bed care for short-term care (vacation, illness, or crisis of caregiver).

Financial Assistance: Private insurance (long-term care benefits) :~ Medicare (hospital care, limitations on long-term care) :~ Medi-Cal in California; Medicaid in other states :~ Family :~ A conference of the elder's children (or other concerned relatives) to determine possibilities of participation in financial assistance.

D. Making the Big Decision

When the time comes that you can no longer care for your parents' needs, in either your home or theirs, even with outside assistance, it is time to assess the options in facility care.

If your parent does not yet need a skilled nursing facility, then assisted living facilities or residential care (board and care) facilities can be a pleasant, gentle transition into more controlled care. In a homelike atmosphere with other elders, there can be the sense of a family of contemporaries, the companionship of a generation in common. Some skilled nursing facilities also have resident-hotel-type quarters where residents have some freedom of movement and access, but are under limited supervision.

Regardless of the type of facility, visit several, using the checklist offered in appendix D to evaluate their quality. Get referrals from people you know and trust, but check each for yourself. Contact the local ombudsman program for information regarding citations or fines from the state for neglect or abuse or other deficiencies. At any skilled nursing facility, yearly inspection reports should be posted and available on request. If a facility refuses access to this material, that fact should be reported to the ombudsman, and you should question whether that facility should remain on your list of prospects.

When you've narrowed the choices to one or two, depending on your elder's ability to make an evaluation without becoming confused, take your elder to visit. Point out the pleasant aspects, the decor, the dining room, the companionship, the accessibility of medical care, and whatever else might appeal to your loved one.

1. Is this a decision my dad can make for himself, given the facts and choices?

If your parent is able to make a choice, the transition will be much smoother. It will be "his own" idea, and therefore more to be tolerated. Allowing that role in decision making retains the elder's sense of control and choice and dignity in determining his future.

2. If my mom is unable to make a decision for herself, am I willing to take that responsibility, and commit to the necessary follow-up to ensure a smooth transition?

There may come a time when you must make the decision. If you make the choice for your parent, there may be times when she blames you for taking over, especially if she has difficulty adjusting to the new regime. Be prepared to stand by your decision, continuing to point out the benefits. Don't try to argue the point or defend your actions. Reassure your elder of your continued love and your understanding of her hesitancy.

If you've evaluated all the available facilities, and have made the choice you feel is the best based on all the factors, you may have to be prepared to accept your own decision despite your elder's objections.

3. Am I making the right decision?

Once again, only you can determine what is the right decision for you, your family, and your loved one. Not everyone — including your loved one — may agree with you. To provide the best chance of successful placement and subsequent care, we recommend using the following plan for a meeting with all personnel involved in the care of your loved one. While section E below outlines the general objectives of the meeting, appendix F offers a specific sample agenda, representative points for discussion, and suggestions for carrying out the meeting.

E. Becoming Cooperative Partners With Long-term Care Facilities

When the time comes to place an elderly loved one in a long-term care facility, it's important that the family, as the consumer, be knowledgeable and prepared to act in the best interest of the elder, hereafter called "resident" (not "patient") by standard industry usage.

Whether the necessity results from sudden trauma or comes after months or years of caring for the loved one independently, emotional and physical factors such as misunderstanding, guilt, fatigue, frustration, and anger can make the family vulnerable to a sense of isolation and loss of control in this new environment.

The following plan was developed through NOBLE's involvement with many families. This concept provides a vehicle for families to exercise their "consumer rights" while assuring the long-term care facility of the family's cooperative intent. The plan consists of the family meeting with all the people involved in the resident's care, for purposes of outlining the expectations and planning the care. The better understanding resulting from this meeting provides better care for the resident from all points of view.

This meeting would take place before or during the placing of a resident; however, the concept could also apply to subsequent problem solving. While a later meeting might take more planning and tactful but emphatic leadership, it could provide improvement in the quality of care.

We encourage families to help set the tone for the relationship between the family and the facility. Establishing this time for all who are involved in the resident's care to share openly and honestly — before any problems arise — allows for non-threatening, non-intimidating dialogue.

When the resident's dignity, care, peace, and security are everyone's foremost purpose, the resulting atmosphere of cooperation benefits all.

Although the facility is required to hold a meeting to discuss care, we suggest the family be proactive in participating, and even requesting a fuller agenda. Scheduling this meeting for all to be present may be difficult, but it's a reasonable request. If done with a professional attitude of optimistic problem solving, the facility should be amenable in the light of benefits for future cooperation. Ideally, the following should be present:

1. Family member, caregiver, responsible party

The responsible family member, often the caregiver, should be prepared to discuss all aspects of the resident's care. This person is the most familiar with the resident's personal needs and habits, and can make helpful suggestions to the facility taking over the care. If the caregiver is too exhausted or stressed by the previous burden of care, the family advocate (#3 below) can take the responsibility of speaking for the caregiver. They should work together to prepare an agenda of points for discussion. List the points in related categories in order to contribute to an orderly, efficient meeting. This not only assures coverage of all items you wish to discuss, but also allows the family to participate equally. Notes on this meeting should be recorded in the care journal mentioned in chapter 11. Honor the time commitment of the others there by being knowledgeable and well prepared.

2. Advocate for Resident

This individual may be the local ombudsman, another family member, a friend, or a clergy person, someone whose only consideration is the objective caring for the expressed wishes and best interest of the resident. He or she can offer ideas from a viewpoint different from the caregiver's.

The ombudsman, available in all states, is an official representative to protect the interests of residents of long-term care facilities and to resolve problems and complaints. Because he or she probably is already familiar with the facility, this person may be a good choice to recruit as your resident's advocate. At any rate, it's wise to get acquainted with this individual before you may need to request help with future problem solving. You can reach your local ombudsman by contacting your county's area agency on aging.

3. Advocate for Family

This person represents vital support for the family-member caregiver, and can be another family member or a friend. The individual must be a well-organized mediator with strong, tactful negotiating skills, able to clarify discussion of a specific point until mutually acceptable resolution is reached. He or she may be the most appropriate to lead the meeting if the caregiver is not a strong leader or needs moral support in this area. This individual should also make notes of the meeting points, any requested actions, etc., for follow-up and for a record of the discussions. These decisions should also be recorded in the journal.

4. Administrator of Facility

As the authority of the facility, this person has power to initiate action, balance your wishes and requests with the facility's rules and regulations, make changes when necessary, and ultimately guarantee a satisfactory lifestyle for the resident. He or she sets the tone for all the facility staff. A spirit of cooperation for the benefit of the resident should be apparent.

5. Medical Professional

This may be the facility staff professional, medical director, director of nursing, or the resident's own physician. Request the presence of the medical professional, whose medical opinion, input, and consequent responsibility for treatment is vital to the success of the meeting as well as the care of the resident.

See appendix F for a representative agenda for such a meeting, adapting it to your own specific concerns.

16 COPING WITH THE DIRTY DOZEN

I've gone to look for myself. If I should return
before I get back, keep me here!

— Anonymous

Who am I? Where am I? Learning to cope, manage, accomplish, make do, "hang in there," persevere — these are the buzz-words of caregivers. Most caregivers have come to terms with the decision to be the caregiver, whether at home, in the elder's home, or overseeing care in a long-term care facility. The question is no longer whether, but how. Most of the questions and frustrations of coping fall into twelve categories that we call the dirty dozen. Looking into each in detail will help you realize that they're common to all of us, and offer you some relief and practical assistance.

1. Coping with Feelings and Attitudes

Feelings are sensory (products of the senses) and therefore responsive or reactive. Some are positive, some negative. Because they're real, they should be acknowledged, but they don't necessarily need to be expressed.

Attitude may be described as a mental outlook or position with regard to a fact. Attitude can, therefore, be conditioned by choice and self-control. Examples:

A. "Mom hurt my feelings with that remark."

Feelings: Hurt — the hurt is real.

Response or Reaction: Nursing the hurt, lashing out, pouting, justification.

Result: Potential for escalation of the situation to frustration, anger, hostility, lack of forgiveness, retaliation.

B. "Dad hurt my feelings with that remark, but…"

Attitude: The hurt is acknowledged, but one's mental position, or attitude, tempers the response.

Response: Dad is hurting and frustrated by his inability to do all that he used to do. I know he loves me and would not choose to hurt me. I choose not to accept the hurt.

Result: Not stuffing unacknowledged hurt beneath the surface where it will fester and break out later, but choosing to hear the hurtful words through the filter of understanding the other person's frustrations.

What if Mom or Dad or Auntie has always been hurtful, never expressing love or appreciation? If you've accepted the role of caregiver, you must choose, for the sake of your own well-being, to respond with the attitude of self-control rather than by acting out feelings.

Author Pearl S. Buck said, "You cannot make yourself feel something you do not feel, but you can make yourself do right in spite of your feelings." An attitude of choice includes choosing to love (love is a choice, not a feeling), choosing to care, to be kind, to be gentle, to respect, to be patient — that's hard, but patience too is a choice.

Rather like a successful marriage, it takes commitment. You can choose to make the relationship a success. Choose to make your parent feel welcome, wanted, loved, and honored. Choose to recognize and credit previous contributions, experience, accomplishments, and family pride. Choose to be generous with praise for what your elder can do. Choose to overlook your negative feelings and those expressed by the elder.

If you lose your temper while trying to master this pattern of attitude above feelings, you're not alone. Choose to walk away from a volatile situation that could degenerate into abusiveness. Start fresh later. Choose to be the first to offer reconciliation if there's a problem, no matter where you think the fault or responsibility lies. No one gains when pride on either side builds cement walls where there should be gardens of understanding.

2. Coping with Awareness

You can ease or altogether avoid many problems associated with relationships with the elderly if you can learn to be aware of and understand changes in temperament or behavior. Sudden radical changes catch our attention immediately, confronting us with the need to solve a problem right now. Many changes come so gradually, however, that it's difficult to recognize any major difference in the personality. But if we're alert to what these changes might be, we then have time to explore the options open to us.

Helen's mother could converse with anyone about art or the latest book she'd read, but thought her son-in-law was her own husband, and accused Helen of trying to steal him from her.

Will's father-in-law could still create beautiful wooden toys, but when Will offered to help him balance his hopelessly confused checkbook, he told all the neighbors Will was trying to steal his money.

Jody's friends saw her mother as a delightful and entertaining luncheon companion, hardly believing Jody's frustrations with her mom's fears and constant complaints. When Aunt Marie stood at the bathroom mirror studying her reflection for long periods of time instead of washing her face and brushing her teeth, Nancy thought Auntie was vain and purposely delaying leaving the house on errands. When Auntie was later diagnosed with Alzheimer's, Nancy learned that the disease sometimes robs its victims of the ability to think through simple tasks of daily personal grooming.

Caregivers who give love and time and effort, often sacrificing personal comfort and privacy to help their elders, frequently report such situations among the most frustrating. Many report guilt when they later realize Mom's fears were legitimate to her, and Dad's cantankerousness was brought about by frustration with his own diminishing capabilities. "If only I had known!" is the cry of many caregivers who might have been able to respond with more understanding and compassion had they been aware that the elder isn't always in control of his or her behavior.

Becoming aware of potential problem areas before they arise can defuse frustrations that lead to conflict. Before reacting to a personality quirk, consider whether it might be related to your elder's own fear or frustration, or a change in physical or mental ability.

Changes in an elder's attitude and behavior are commonly noticed in many areas: Mom becomes forgetful, misplaces or hides things, neglects her appearance, personal hygiene, and usual activities and duties, and becomes abrupt and demanding. Dad becomes reclusive, or demands inclusion in every activity, has unusual fears and obsessions, becomes suspicious and accusatory, uses unacceptable language, forgets social restraints and courtesies, loses understanding of money handling, changes eating habits, sleeps too much or too little, wanders, snoops, and doesn't respect privacy.

The list goes on and on. You could add your own observations. The point is to increase your own awareness of changes, in order to be prepared to respond with levelheadedness and understanding. Even when you don't really understand, it's important to keep your own dignity and that of your elder intact. (The dignity of the caregiver is discussed in paragraph 11.)

3. Coping with Family Involvement

Even with the best of intentions, and the best of plans, there'll still be times of frustration and conflict. The ideas presented here primarily affect the role of the caregiver's family when the elder is living with the family.

The commitment to caring for an elder at home should take into consideration the needs of the immediate family, but the caregiver (and spouse, if applicable) is the decision maker and must make the final decision. All members of the family need to understand that it's a decision you're choosing to make, even if you feel you have no other choice, and it could be a long-term decision. Save yourself the frustration of rehashing arguments about whether the decision should have been made. Adjustments and compromises will be necessary. Schedules won't be as easily established or changed as before. Attempt to "be there" for your children's activity schedules, but help them learn the give-and-take of balancing wants with needs. Spontaneity to pick up and go will be curtailed. Establish a ground rule specifying that only positive problem solving discussions take place. Recruit the kids' creative suggestions.

Sometimes, you'll have to make unpopular decisions. Try to maintain an open, cooperative atmosphere, where the children learn the value of teamwork and compromise. Offer flexible terms of negotiation, but see that negotiations are carried out as quickly and equitably as possible. Don't trap yourself in promises that can backfire, just to ease the immediate situation. Be realistic.

4. Coping with Responsibility

In chapter 11 we also discussed the need for mutual understanding and settling the issue of responsibility for the care of the elder within the extended family. Assuming that the role of caregiver has now come to you and your immediate family, you might need to further assess and clarify to handle the ever-changing circumstances requiring decisions.

As far as is possible, allow your loved one to retain as much responsibility for himself as he is able. My dad was able to handle the business aspect of his life — checkbook, banking, insurance, and appointments — and retain the dignity in that. But unfamiliar or unexpected details panicked him. For example, Medicare statements outlining treatments and providers of services look like bills, but aren't. In Dad's mind, these were bills that had to be paid, and he worried whether there was money to cover them. Other caregivers report that advertising materials for goods or services also look like bills because they include order blanks. Health fund drives, broadcasting fund drives, religious fund drives, unsolicited "gifts" of stamps, calendars, stationery, etc., all tend to appeal to loyalty and generosity, and are easily misunderstood.

Allow Mom to make as many choices as possible in determining her current welfare. She may choose a dress you don't care for, but if she loves it and it makes her feel good, and it isn't inappropriate, don't impose your choice on her. Just because she needs physical assistance in living arrangements, don't assume that she's unable to make other decisions with wisdom and experience. There may come a time, because of diminishing understanding or capability, when you must take over responsibilities your loved one previously handled for herself.

One dad, in complete control of his mental faculties before a major surgery, resisted, but finally reluctantly signed a power of attorney enabling a trusted daughter to handle his business matters if necessary during his recuperation. A stroke immediately following the surgery left him permanently unable to speak, write, or even indicate his opinions.

Offer your assistance tactfully, as a benefit, not a seizing of control. It's wise to have previously arranged for alternate signatures on a bank account or a power of attorney, which allows the designee to handle business affairs. But this can be a touchy subject, one that many elders may have difficulty accepting. Unfortunately, it's also an area in which financial abuse of the elder can occur. Perhaps an objective friend or advisor, trusted by the elder, can help explain the benefits of prearranging the handling of business. Always place yourself in your loved one's position. *What if this were happening to me?* Reassure your loved one that this measure simply allows you to help him or her through the often confusing aspects of financial matters.

Some concerned elders want to talk about death and final arrangements. We sometimes shy away from the subject, thinking we're reassuring them of long life — "Oh, Mom, you're going to live forever!" — when our own hesitancy to talk about the death of a parent is the issue. Many elders know their time is becoming limited, and they need to settle the issues now. Be prepared to accept their reality. In so doing you give them the gift of peace of mind, and you'll learn details that will help you make those final arrangements when the time comes.

5. Coping with Role Reversal

"Sarah, I'm hungry. When's dinner? What's for dinner?"

"Mother, we just got up. Breakfast will be ready in a few minutes."

"I don't want breakfast. It's dinnertime. I don't like eggs."

"But, Mom..."

"Well, I'm not having breakfast. I'm not going to eat."

Does role reversal really happen? You bet it does, and it can throw you for a loop till you realize what's happening. We fight against giving up the nurturing we ourselves still want, in order to nurture this vaguely familiar child in our parent's body.

As long as our parents live, we still want and expect them to be our parents. The unexpected slipping from one role into another catches us off guard and keeps us on edge.

But your mom may be there the next morning, hungry for eggs again. The first evidence of role reversal isn't always permanent, but it can be a sign of what's ahead. The frustration occurs in that slippery time of never knowing which role Mom is in at any given moment. Like the Boy Scouts, it's wise to "Be prepared." The frightening thing is that you don't know what to be prepared for. Eggs and breakfast aren't so difficult to deal with, but next time, Mom may head down the road, looking for her mama.

At this point of recognizing role reversal, we actually begin the grieving process of separation associated with death. Our parent is no longer as we knew him or her. It's not easy, but now is the time when you must accept what is and move on to what must be. You must begin to accept your new role of providing the care and nurturing and making the decisions associated with being a parent to your loved one.

Sometimes you'll make the right decision. Relish it. Remember it. It may or may not work the next time. If it doesn't, don't punish yourself. You're in trial-and-error territory. Try to be as kind to yourself as you're trying to be to the beloved elder in your care.

6. Coping with Dignity

Retaining the elder's dignity is probably the most important thing you can do. It may take some creative thinking, but choosing to make it a priority will go a long way toward preserving the success of your relationship.

The current trend toward idolizing youth, beauty, and fitness has left many of our elders not only without dignity and honor, but also without advocates. Elders who are facing new living arrangements, giving up their own homes, moving to a retirement center, an adult child's home, or a long-term care facility, have fragile egos and feelings. Whatever the reason for the change — illness, enforced retirement, diminished abilities — the need for radical change in lifestyle usually results in a traumatic assault against already vulnerable sensitivities. Mother may have been a very capable business executive before retirement snuck up on her, leaving her feeling useless. Dad may have been a vigorous outdoorsman used to outwitting nature at every turn, before a stroke left him unable to step out the back door without help.

Dignity should be a given in every person's life. Unfortunately, it isn't. Dignity should mean free choice, freedom from embarrassment, freedom from mental, physical, and financial abuse, and respect for each individual as a human being regardless of his condition.

In a long-term care facility, my mother was occasionally bathed and taken to the bathroom by a young male aide her grandson's age. She was dressed and undressed without the privacy of a curtain or closed door. She was confined in a wheelchair for too long at a stretch. Her bathroom wasn't checked for cleanliness often enough. She often had to wait too long to be taken to the bathroom, or to be changed if she had an accident. She was handled roughly, with evident bruising. Her personal belongings, even her dentures, disappeared. In each of these situations she had no choice.

Indignities can also occur in our own homes when we get too busy, too rushed, or too tired and overworked to feel empathy with the one we're caring for. We can't teach dignity, just as we can't teach love and caring, but we must require accountability for common courtesies. The accumulation of small indignities can also be powerful in eroding a person's sense of well-being and control over her own life, resulting in shattered self-respect, withdrawal, and depression.

During the time my parents lived with us, there was a period in which I also nursed my husband's father during his final illness. He was a proud man who hated the condition his illness had brought on him. He was used to being in control of his life, and it was hard for him to accept personal care from me. I'd grown up knowing, respecting, and loving him, and didn't want anything to interfere with our mutual respect. His obvious discomfort with what I had, of necessity, to do in caring for him made me uncomfortable. I tried to start each morning on a happy note, but it became harder to create one-sided pleasantries.

One morning as I opened the drapes, I spontaneously said, "Good morning, Sam. It's a beautiful day." I wondered where that came from. His name was Alwyn, but I called him Grandpop. There was no visible response, but I felt better, so next morning I tried it again with a chuckle in my voice. Still no response. But because it lightened my mood, I said it again the third morning.

"Good morning, Samantha," Grandpop replied gruffly. I nearly fell over. That became our greeting every morning. It served to lighten our relationship and our daily activities, and, I realized, it created an atmosphere of nurse to patient instead of daughter-in-law to father-in-law, which eased the embarrassment of the nursing care.

Retaining and reinforcing personal dignity can be one of the most powerful therapies you can offer your elder. Make it your choice! As a resulting benefit, you'll experience a strengthening of your own dignity.

7. Coping with Idiosyncrasies

There's a story of a young bride who cut a piece off each end of a ham before placing it in the roasting pan. Puzzled, her new husband asked her why. "Because Mom always did it that way." The next time the couple visited her parents, they asked her mother about it. She replied, "My mother always fixed her hams that way." Finally, at Christmas, the entire clan gathered at Grandma's. Sure enough, she prepared a ham, slicing off each end before placing it in the roasting pan. "Grandma," the young bride asked, "I've asked Mom and she doesn't know. Why do we have to cut off the ends of the ham before baking it?" Grandma laughed. "I don't know why you and your mom cut off the ends. I do it because my pan isn't big enough to hold the whole thing!"

Eccentricities, oddities, peculiarities, habits, quirks — we all have them, and not necessarily because we're old. Some idiosyncrasies are endearing, some are weird, and some are irritating, especially when they're someone else's. And when we're facing the other aspects of caregiving, and dealing with the mysteries of aging personalities, they can become the "last straw."

Telling the same stories over and over. And over! (Till you know the stories and remember the names, dates, and incidents better than the one telling it, and are tempted to break in to finish the story.)

Asking the same questions over and over. And over!

Fixing the sofa pillows or folding the napkins just a certain way.

Saving things: rubber bands, plastic margarine cups, pencil stubs, plastic bags, broken shoestrings.

Draping wet dishtowels all around the kitchen; ironing clean dishtowels.

Hurrying to get the mail before anyone else can.

Washing paper plates to use again.

Idiosyncrasies are as individual as the people who have them. If we try to understand or figure them out or change them we run into frustrations. If they're just harmless quirks, allow the elder to "own" his or her own idiosyncrasies.

Consider the impact over time. Does it really matter, in the long run, whether Dad saves rubber bands, or Mom washes paper plates or drapes wet towels around the kitchen? You can discreetly gather laundry or dispose of the paper goods later. There's a popular slogan: "Don't sweat the small stuff. (It's all small stuff!)" But caregivers know it isn't all small stuff. If Grandma loses the mail or hides important things, other solutions need to be found. On one of the last visits to her mother's home, Elaine observed Marie leafing through a two-foot stack of old magazines till she finally pulled out a twenty-dollar bill to take shopping. After Marie was hospitalized with a stroke, and it was known she'd never be able to live at home again, Elaine remembered Marie's unusual "banking system." Leafing through the stacks of magazines destined for the recycle bin, she found eighty dollars.

8. Coping with Fear

Many idiosyncrasies stem from fear: fear of change, of the unknown, of losing control of one's own life, of losing one's health, of death.

Sitting up all night for fear of dying in bed.

Scotch-taping the curtains to the wall all around the window "so no one can peek in."

Refusing to eat because "someone is trying to poison me."

Becoming suspicious, argumentative, uncooperative: "They're whispering about me," when in reality, the elder denied being deaf and refused to consider a hearing aid.

My mother had a terror of being buried alive. In her childhood she had heard of a person, thought dead, who awoke and sat up in the mortuary. I repeatedly promised her that we would not allow her body to be prepared for final disposition for three days after she died. We kept that promise. Though I was embarrassed to ask it of the funeral director, he accepted it as Mom's wish and our promise, and he graciously fulfilled the request.

Gently and repeatedly addressing the fears with affirmation and a loving attitude may help restore confidence. Caregivers, overworked and overtired, may have difficulty being patient. Try to see the person through the eyes of her own fears. Realize that rational thinking probably isn't possible. It's hardest when the accusations and suspicions are directed at you or one of your family. Although the suspicions and accusations Mom directed at me stung, I could overlook them. But when she turned on my husband, who'd shared in her care for twenty-five years, I tried to make clear that this was untrue and couldn't be tolerated.

Nothing I said could convince her, and this was the beginning of the end of my ability to care for her at home.

If you suspect that your loved one's level of fear might indicate para-noiac or psychotic proportions, which isn't uncommon, inform your physician. Medication can at times be very effective in reducing this symptom (disturbing to both patient and family), and can make the difference between safely staying at home and institutionalization.

You can't be prepared to recognize and ease every fear that may assail your loved one. It's not really what you say to alleviate her fear, it's the way you address it; your tone of voice, your quiet manner. It's a continu-ous job of reassurance, for which there's no preparation. You just have to keep reinforcing, and know that it's probably going to get worse.

Your elder's fears may seem trivial and therefore strain your patience, but every fear is very real to your loved one and, from her viewpoint, needs to be addressed right now! It takes patience, persistence, and love, even when you don't feel like it. See paragraph 12 regarding "love when you don't feel like it."

The result of not addressing her fears is an agitated, frightened, angry, hurt human being. Sometimes, all that's needed is for the elder to see you making an attempt to remove the fear. When all else fails, try a hug. If that doesn't work, then just be there, so she's not alone at the moments when she's most afraid.

9. Coping with Frustration

Frustration is probably at the root of all coping problems. Frustrations are inevitable, but how we handle them determines the climate of success in dealing with our aging loved ones. When we're raising our children, we all have a tendency to want to "make it all better." In the same way, when we find ourselves parenting our parents, we want to make all their problems and frustrations disappear. But we can't make everything all better. We can't change the elder's reactions to exasperating situations, but when we change our expectations of them and of ourselves, we can ease the tensions surrounding the problems.

Usually, frustration results from thwarted desires, plans, or expectations, or a clash of wills, personalities, or methods of problem solving. It's a creative challenge to resolve problems with increasing frequency and decreasing frustration. Keep in mind that easing your elder's frustration level also eases your own.

Humor can defuse many tense situations. One caregiver reported that after months of turmoil in the household, with everyone in the family at odds with one another, they finally realized that Grandma was playing one member of the family against another, constantly agitating. Then she'd go off to her room and shut the door. They recognized that her temperament was unlikely to change. Understanding that helped them not to react with one another, and gentled their reactions to her. They were able to turn it into a private family joke with each other, saying, "Grandma's not really happy till everyone else is in an uproar."

I like to use the analogy of a box tied up with ribbon, sitting on your closet shelf. I suggest you actually prepare such a box, a pretty one with lovely ribbons. When you're faced with frustrations you're not yet prepared to solve, take some time out, write the situation on a piece of paper, place it in the box, and tie the bow. Tightly! Writing it down, frustration and all, relieves some of the tension and articulates your feelings. Placing it in the box prevents the psychologically dangerous reflex of "stuffing" your feelings internally, only to have them erupt later, unsolved and more damaging. Instead, when you feel calmer, take down the box, untie the bow, take out one of your written frustrating situations, and evaluate it.

What about this situation frustrates me? Thwarted desires, plans, or expectations? Are my desires and plans legitimate? Is there any other way I can accomplish my goals? Do I expect too much of Mom? Of myself? Is it a clash of personalities or wills? Were we always like this? Why does the situation frustrate me? Am I trying to prove something? Is there something from our past relationship that I'm trying to get even for? Am I getting some reward from trying to prove a point with this dear old soul who used to do so much for me? Or maybe she didn't do so much for me. Is that why I'm frustrated? Am I punishing her for a perceived lack in our past?

Put yourself in your loved one's shoes. As an exercise, try stuffing your ears with cotton or covering your eyes. Try using only the left side of your body, as if the right side were paralyzed from a stroke. Try sitting upright in a hard chair for a period of time. When you need to go to the bathroom, consider what it would be like if you had to wait forty-five more minutes for help. Think about what it's like to have an aide of the opposite sex undress you before bedtime. Consider your loved one's frustration at not being in control of her own life. Consider her fear of the unknown. Is there something you can do to alleviate the fears and frustrations? A soothing word, a smile, a gentle touch, a bit of the golden rule, a capitulation to his or her way of wanting to do things, or something even more tangible — a change of plans to really make Mom feel like "Queen for a Day." Just once in a while — would that be so difficult?

Evaluate the options. Jot them down. Now place your note back in the frustration box and retie the ribbon. Try the new ideas for a few days. Think of it as a gift you're willing to offer your loved one. Smile a lot.

You may never get to all the frustrations in the box, and that's okay. And some days you may not even have time to physically write down the situations. The box can be symbolic. Do it mentally. Choose to lay it aside. The benefit comes from freeing yourself of the unnecessary baggage. You can get on with today, with the promise that you'll think about it tomorrow. This is not procrastination; it's survival. Face it and solve it when you can. Some of the frustrations may cease to be frustrations when the pressure is off.

10. Coping with Guilt

How do I feel guilty? Let me count the ways.

A. Roy feels guilty because he had to place his mother in a long-term care facility against her wishes.

B. Ellen feels guilty that she couldn't take care of Roy's mother in their home.

C. Sara feels guilty when she goes out to lunch with a friend without taking her mom along.

D. David feels guilty when he visits his widowed mother, who still lives in her own home. He visits twice a week, but feels he should go more often.

E. Elmer feels guilty for shouting at his young son to hurry, when it was Grandpa who was so slow getting to the car.

F. Laura feels guilty for asking her fifteen-year-old to share a room with his six-year-old brother to make room for Grandpa.

G. Angie feels guilty for wanting to run out of the room when her mother starts complaining about the children's afternoon noisiness when Grandma wants to nap.

H. Susan feels guilty for shutting the door to her bedroom when she and her husband retire for the evening.

And the list goes on, and on, and on.

Every caregiver has grappled with guilt — real guilt and false guilt. Every caregiver must learn to deal with both. There's no room for either. There's no excuse for either. Now, doesn't that make you feel guilty?

Take a "True-False" test. Reread the list above and mark each one T for true guilt or F for false guilt.

Now let's look at the examples in more detail.

A. Roy considered every option for the level of care his mother needs, then made the only choice possible. Even though his mom doesn't like the decision, he has no reason to carry guilt.

B. Ellen works full time, has two busy teenagers and a small house, and has never had a close relationship with Roy's mother. She has no reason to carry guilt.

C. Sara is a homemaker caring for her mom at home daily. Sara needs time to "be Sara" with her own friends, and not just "daughter Sara." She has no reason to carry guilt.

D. David is a single, only child who feels responsible for his mother since his dad's death. He travels frequently in his business, but still manages to see Mom twice a week. Yet she insists it isn't enough. Her complaint would probably be the same even if he came more often. David has no reason to carry guilt.

E. Elmer is frustrated with Grandpa, and though he wouldn't shout at his father, he thinks by yelling at his son, Grandpa will get the point. The guilt he feels is true guilt, but can quickly be eliminated when Elmer apologizes to his son for taking his frustration out on him. Of course, this doesn't give Elmer license to shout at Grandpa instead. He might ease the problem by allowing more time than necessary to get to their destination, or giving Grandpa an earlier departure time than is actually needed, so Grandpa doesn't feel rushed.

F. Sometimes families simply have to learn the give-and-take of shared living quarters, provided that's the best or only option. If, instead of feeling guilty, Laura could put her energies into creatively adapting the available space, several valuable lessons about responsibility might result. (See discussion in the previous section on Family Involvement, #3 above.) Creative room division, involving her sons in the planning, establishing "ground rules," making appropriate concessions to the older son — all might create a better atmosphere. But Laura need not carry guilt for doing what's necessary for Grandpa's care.

G. Angie feels trapped by a repetitive behavior that's unlikely to change. It's reasonable that Grandma needs a nap. It's also reasonable that children are sometimes noisy. Flexibility is a sanity-saving asset. A quiet time for Angie and the kids could become a precious time-out for crafts or projects, board games, reading together or separately, a trip to the library, the park playground, or any other activity or "field trip" that would give Grandma time for a nap. Conversely, Grandma, with more available discretionary time, might be persuaded to nap at another time, and might need to realize that in a home with small children there will sometimes be noise. Angie doesn't need to carry guilt about children being children, nor put guilt on them as long as reasonable courtesies are observed.

H. In a shared living situation, the elder is not a guest to be entertained. Susan and her husband need time alone together. She needn't feel guilty for shutting the bedroom door, and if necessary, installing a lock.

Only example E represents true guilt. True guilt is for something, intentional or unintentional, that has caused hurt or pain or hardship. False guilt is guilt assumed for things that are neither your responsibility nor in your power to change.

Make a list of all the things you've been feeling guilty about. Examine your feelings and try to identify the source of each one. Mark a T or an F by each item you listed. If you evaluate your list objectively, most of the things on it are probably false guilt. Mark a line through all those things. Determine to dismiss them and refuse to pick them up again. Now look at the remaining items. If there are reasons for true guilt, determine an action to make them right. Is an apology needed? Do it. Can something be done to alleviate the situation? Do it — now, or as soon as possible — then forget it. Make the decision and the choice to set things right.

No guilt should last longer than it takes to identify its authenticity and deal with or dismiss it. For your own sanity, do it.

11. Coping with Caring for the Caregiver

Caregivers are often multifunctional. You've seen the lists of professional tasks that "ordinary" women perform: housewife, career woman, mother, nurse, chauffeur, errand runner, tutor, secretary, chef, entertainer, companion, lover, cleaning lady, laundress, seamstress, and so on. When a man becomes the primary caregiver — and the numbers are increasing — he's not exempt from the array of responsibilities. Add all the duties of caring for another generation (again, whether at home or in long-term care), and you see that many caregivers feel they can never stop for a break or see to their own legitimate needs. You sometimes feel, mistakenly, that you're indispensable. It's a formidable undertaking, but as with any efficient piece of machinery, proper upkeep and maintenance is a must. You have got to take care of you. You owe it to yourself; you owe it to your family; you owe it to your elder.

Deal with guilt. If you're the caregiver, don't let anyone else lay guilt on you, and don't lay it on yourself. If another family member is the primary caregiver, help that person not to assume guilt.

Determine the areas in which you need nurturing — physical, mental, emotional, and spiritual. List the things that nurture you in each area. Separate your list into categories depending on the chunks of time necessary to accomplish them, from five minutes to a whole weekend away. Find ways to work the smaller pleasures into your day, every day.

As with small children, use the time when your elder is napping to do things for yourself. Take a long bath, do your nails, make some lemonade, read a book, sit in the sun and listen to the birds, or take a nap. If it's therapy for you, and not a chore, go out to the garage and putter, polish your car or your golf clubs, work on a project, or pull a few weeds. Do not do the laundry or scrub the bathroom or take out the trash. There'll be time for all that. For now, treat yourself.

When you're feeling shredded from the constant calls for your attention, it may be necessary and appropriate to respond, "I'll be there in just a minute (or five)." Then, when you can reasonably break into what you're doing, attend to the elder's request, but don't abuse this "grace period" of delay.

There may be several ways to take a break away from home. Sue, with a fairly active elder, found another caregiver with an active elder and they traded mornings, bringing the elders together to visit, sit in the park, or go for a drive, while the other caregiver enjoyed a break. Lois tried a similar routine but found it was more trouble than it was worth. It took longer to get her mom ready and out; it didn't seem to entertain Mom, and it added stress to Lois' day to include another person to look after even for a short time. Janet's sister, who worked during the week, agreed to come every other Saturday morning so Janet and her husband could go out to lunch together.

It won't all be positive. At considerable expense, one desperate caregiver arranged a weekend at a board and care for her mom while she and her husband had a weekend, also at considerable expense, at a nearby favorite place. The first evening, they luxuriated in the privacy, the pool, and the lovely restaurant. She found herself crying all the second day as she realized she had to go home the third. She was also worried about how Mom was handling the weekend. She tried to laugh at herself for crying, but realized she'd waited too long to take the break.

We discussed extended family involvement in chapter 11. If there's extended family, other children or grandchildren of the elder, it may be wise to make a specific request, and specify a time. Don't wait for someone to volunteer. Your request may be met with refusal; if you can't negotiate a compromise, you need to learn to accept that without bitterness. Check the resources offered in chapter 15 for help in finding paid companions or even volunteers to help free you for your own respite.

Don't make yourself or your family ill from holding in the difficulties. Share with someone you trust, an understanding friend, or even a professional, someone who's not involved personally. Make an appointment with Dad's doctor, or a clergy person, for a private time when you can perhaps get some insight into your situation and learn positive approaches to solving problems.

It may seem obvious, but it's often overlooked — keep yourself well-groomed. When you feel you're shut in at home with your elder, it's easy to let personal grooming slide. How many of us have been caught answering the door looking unkempt? It's an old adage, but true, that when you look your best you feel better. We've already discussed the psychological advantages of helping the elder maintain good grooming, but it's just as true for the caregiver. You not only feel better, but also you project an image of calmness and self-control.

Bottom line? You're not only caregiving for the elder, but also for the caregiver — yourself. You deserve it. You'll function more efficiently and calmly when you nurture your own physical, mental, spiritual, and emotional needs. Even taking this into consideration, there'll be days when you feel put-upon and martyred. You've already discovered there are daily ups and downs. On days when everything goes well, the residual "fallout" refreshes everyone. There'll be dark days when nothing seems to work, and there's no light anywhere. Try to dismiss them. Don't carry hurts and grudges to bed where they'll nag, robbing you of rest and peace of mind. Learn the art of doing what you can and then releasing the rest.

12. Coping with Love

Do you have to cope with love? Coping sounds like a burden. Isn't love a given? I was always surrounded with it, and I loved both my parents deeply. Life was real; it wasn't always a bowl of cherries, but we faced the pits and dealt with them. Because I grew up in a happy home, I assumed, perhaps naively, that everyone would naturally love, care for, and cherish their parents or other family elders.

It's easy to love lovable people, but some people grow up in homes where love is not expressed openly, where accomplishments are the basis for approval, where demands and expectations obscure any expressions of love. Unfortunately, many even experience abuse at the hands of parents. Surely we can't ask those people to love and cherish and protect their elders, can we?

Family background influences every decision. No two families experience the same history, genetics, environment, or ethics. Positive backgrounds can lead to positive feelings, but sometimes the love one experiences in a positive background can lead to negative feelings because of a sense of obligation, which can carry its own guilt trip. Obviously, negative backgrounds can lead to negative feelings because of feeling no responsibility to what one perceived as an unfavorable family history. But a negative history can also lead to positive determination to change the cycle and overcome past disadvantages. If we can learn to "accentuate the positive" and "eliminate the negative" by dealing with it, everyone benefits.

Love is a choice. Too often, we can't bring out our feelings of love, and so feel guilty that we don't "love" our elder when he or she is being difficult. But love chooses to overlook the quarrelsomeness, complaining, and volatile changes in behavior. One caregiver reported taking her mother-in-law into their home out of loyalty to her husband. Although motivated by thoughts of duty, a sense of it being the right thing to do, she confessed no love for this woman who had been a gossiping, self-centered, complaining troublemaker most of her life. Elaine felt guilty because she didn't love her mother-in-law. Things were very difficult for months; the breakthrough came when Elaine realized she had been choosing to do the loving things, the right things, even without the feelings.

Love chooses what's right for the other person. Love chooses to be patient, to be kind, to put the other person first. Love chooses not to react with anger, to overlook minor irritations and not dwell on them. Love chooses to find ways to solve major problems, and not to keep track of the other's faults. Love chooses to protect, to trust, to remain hopeful. Love chooses to hang in there and never give up.

And in the choosing, love eventually discovers it does truly feel love.

17 You'll Never Walk Alone

In the early days of my advocacy I did so much by instinct alone that I often felt entirely alone. I wondered if anything I could do would have any impact at all in the vast wilderness of elder advocacy. As I began to meet other people — and everywhere I told my story, others would relate similar situations — I realized that I wasn't alone. But few of us knew what others were doing; it was by trial and error and happenstance that we discovered common bonds, common purposes, and ways of supporting one another.

Are you asking similar questions? What can one person do? What difference can it make? Why bother?

Perhaps some of the following stories will encourage you as they have me.

Life Is Not Just a Box of Chocolates

Her name was Frances Jones. I never met her. She was a voice — a warm, soothing, caring voice. She'd heard me on a radio program and called to ask for advice about a minor problem she'd encountered concerning her sister, who was in a local long-term care facility. It was about a box of chocolates sent for Valentine's Day that didn't get delivered. I didn't consider her dilemma minor at all. The phone calls flew back and forth.

The nursing home said no candy had ever arrived. But it had been sent by UPS, which provided receipts signed by a nursing home employee. After some discussion, excuses, challenges, and proofs, Frances was eventually given a check for the amount of the candy plus the shipping charges. She bought a new box and handed it to her sister for a belated Valentine's Day celebration.

I called Frances from my office occasionally, just to see how things were going. Despite her limited income, Frances began calling me, particularly at holiday times.

"Honey, it's Frances," in that warm voice, concerned for my welfare, always sensitive to my moods. "Are you doing all right? Are you getting enough rest?"

Then the calls stopped. I knew she was receiving treatment for a medical condition. Apprehensive, I tried a number of times to reach her, with no success. Finally, her daughter answered the phone. Frances had passed away a few days before.

There's a Frances-sized hole in my heart. She was a warm, generous lady on a fixed income, who probably didn't think of herself as a crusader against elder abuse, but her encouragement helped me face many of the frustrating days I went through while trying to help other families. So her gift was multiplied many times over.

One person *can* make a difference!

"I Know You Can Help Me"

By the time his father passed away, Rick Campbell had seen enough of nursing homes to swear he'd never set foot in one again. Relieved to be closing that chapter, he was looking forward to a newer, fresher phase of his life. But a plea from a woman in his church changed all that. Her mother, who spoke no English, resided in a nursing home and missed receiving communion. "I know you can help me," she implored.

Rick couldn't get the woman off his mind. He asked his priest about the possibility of a layperson being trained, and from that encounter, Rick became qualified to give communion. A new ministry was born. Even though the language barrier created difficulties, the more common language of the elements of communion allowed a greater communication.

"Other people saw me serving communion and wanted to take part too. The sense of aloneness of some of these people in long-term care is overwhelming. Some have no visitors, no family. Some have outlived their friends and relatives. And some are comparatively young — victims of debilitating diseases or accidents that have left them unable to live at home. These young residents are housed and treated with the same regimen as the elderly, which is particularly discouraging for people whose adult lives were just beginning when they were sidelined by circumstances of accident or disease over which they had no control.

"Why can't we have these young people housed together in separate facilities, or at least separate wings, providing the amenities for as normal a life as possible? They'd like to have access to music and entertainment, clothing, menus, and even daily schedules to suit their tastes."

Rick's dream is to see such facilities made available to younger people. Rick still experiences the frustrations of trying to make things better within a sometimes-difficult system. But he's also experienced the joys of accomplishment. He was nominated for the Heroes of the Heart Award from Children's Hospital of Orange County.

"I'll probably never give up advocating for these people. Just when I think the load is lightening, I find new hands to hold. And I can't say no. Whether or not I can change the big picture, it takes so little to make a difference in their lives. Anyone can do that."

One person *can* make a difference!

A Voice Out of the Night

Who listens to the radio in the middle of the night? Many people do, and they even call the stations! One sleepless night, Janice Karich heard my advocacy mentioned on a show discussing issues concerning the elderly. Janice's experiences with the facility where her grandmother had been made her immediately sympathetic and supportive of NOBLE's work. Although she was ill, she offered to do anything she could do from her home to help — research, mailings, phoning. She became a one-woman clipping service, providing our files with newspaper and magazine items and articles about elder abuse. She made phone calls and wrote letters supporting our work. And she became a one-woman support system for me, allowing me to release frustrations long-distance, when I chose not to do so with close family and friends.

Janice finally succumbed to her own illness, but she'd been a constant gift to me.

One person *can* make a difference!

"Anything…anything…"

When Pat Valdez entered my office at NOBLE, I read in her eyes a steely determination that only hinted at the trauma she had experienced. Like many of us involved in this work, Pat experienced elder abuse first-hand while overseeing her aunt's care. In an eighteen-month period, her aunt lived in six long-term care facilities where she experienced abuse, neglect, and over-medication, till she had to be sent to a psychiatric facility for detoxification. Then Pat had extreme difficulty finding a bed in a long-term care facility that would accept a transfer from a psychiatric facility. According to the administrator of one facility she applied to, it's common for there to be "no available beds" for residents coming out of psychiatric facilities.

Pat's aunt had died by the time we met, but the hurt and outrage were still very close to the surface. She offered to do anything needed for the office, typing at home after her own workday ended.

When I began making presentations for various groups and organizations, Pat agreed to tell her story and allowed us to use the pictures of her aunt's abuse. She testified before a public hearing called by California Assemblyman Gil Ferguson. She became an invaluable member of the board of directors of NOBLE. Her attitude was, "If you ever need me for anything—anything, call me. I'll do it."

One person *can* make a difference!

It Had to Be FATE

"I believe you," said the voice on the other end of the line. "I've been there. Nothing surprises me anymore." I felt her empathy immediately.

That was my introduction to Carole Herman, the founder of FATE (Foundation Aiding the Elderly), in Sacramento, California. After her aunt died in a long-term care facility, following gross neglect of decubitis ulcers, Carole established FATE, where she has been making a difference for more than thirty years. She is a dedicated advocate for the elderly, educating herself, then others, in the maze of officialdom regulating care facilities throughout the state, pushing for reform, for enforcement of present laws, for necessary new laws, and encouraging novice advocates like me. Having "been there, done that," Carole was unhesitatingly generous with helpful suggestions. As we realized our goals and operating styles were compatible, we served on one another's boards of directors.

Every advocate needs, but doesn't always have, personal contact with another advocate. The mutual encouragement, strength, and support are benefits no one else can provide with the same degree of empathy. Carole is a wife, mother, grandmother, and the vice president of her own company. She's extraordinary in what she does, but ordinary in that she's one individual doing what she can, to the best of her ability. In her, as in so many others who've experienced the outrage of elder abuse, runs that common thread of needing to do something, and to pass along any help that's in her power to give.

"Closure (of your own case) is really only the beginning of advocacy for others," she says.

One person *can* make a difference!

The Journey is Not Complete

Elder abuse respects no one. It didn't matter that Sandra Hagan was a strong, articulate, bank vice president who'd placed her mother in what she had considered the "finest skilled-care facility in the area." Her mother's death was attributed to neglect of sepsis (major infection) caused by dry gangrene.

As with so many people who came to my office, Sandra knew she needed to do something to have closure. Her route has taken several paths. At her church, she taught a course titled "Honor Your Father and Mother, for Middle Adults Who Love and Care for Older Adults"

(© 1989 by Graded Press, Nashville, TN). The course investigates various aspects of "the sandwich generation" dealing with eldercare.

The local Department of Health Services, Licensing and Certification
office had issued a Class B Citation with a $1000 fine against the facility
where her mother died, but this was an unacceptably light judgment in
view of her mother's death.

As was her right, Sandra contested the original finding, and eventually
a Class A Citation carrying a penalty of $10,000 was issued against the
facility. Because Sandra felt no certainty there would be real change, she
brought a successful lawsuit against the facility.

The journey continues. Sandra is currently executive director of
NOBLE.

One person *can* make a difference!

The Dream Team

When Randa Mendenhall returned to the United States after
several years abroad, she arbitrarily decided to seek employment in
Washington, D.C. She had defined her dream job as working in one
of the foreign ambassadorial offices or an international corporation,
where she could use her proficiency in several languages. But after
forty-five interviews in two and a half weeks, that dream job hadn't yet
materialized.

Then came a call from a friend who worked on the White House staff
saying that Mrs. Pat Nixon's office had a position for her. At the age of
twenty-four, Randa was hired as social correspondent to the First Lady!

Seventeen years later, another friend encouraged her to apply as a
volunteer on Mrs. Barbara Bush's staff. Although she was working full
time, Randa retained one day a week for volunteer work, and for four
great years, she worked in the special projects office for Mrs. Bush.

It was Randa Mendenhall who responded so graciously to my correspondence with Mrs. Bush about my advocacy work with NOBLE,
bringing it to Mrs. Bush's attention, being the intermediary for our
correspondence, and opening the doors for an invitation to the White

House. That appointment has lent great credibility to NOBLE's work, and for that I'm very grateful.

Not everyone can work in the White House.

But one person *can* make a difference!

We've Been Walking Alone ... Together

I can't address this to you by name — I never knew your name. I wanted to know. I wanted to confront you, to demand reasons and answers. But my reasoning side knew I was too full of rage to handle such an encounter.

But you changed my life. Nothing was the same after that day so long ago. My precious mother was no longer there for me, and would never be there again. It was a big change going through the frustrations of trying to see that nothing like this ever again happened to anyone's mother — even yours. It was a change meeting people I'd never had any reason to meet before. It was a change becoming bold enough to speak out about the unacknowledged problem of abuse of our elder generation. It was a change learning the ropes of advocacy work, facing government representatives, trying to work with industry representatives, hearing the heartbreaking stories of far too many families who'd experienced far too many incidents similar to mine.

With the help of many others, I've been able to help many families. In the process of establishing NOBLE, I heard from hundreds of families in thirty-eight states, detailing all sorts of abuse by people like you all over the US. And I know my experiences represent just the tip of the iceberg of a chilling national disgrace.

It's been years since you began these changes in my life, since my mother died six weeks after you beat her. And now, after all that's happened in these past years, I sense a new change in my life. You're involved in that too. It's not complete yet. I'm not sure it ever will be. I'm told that for my own sake it must become complete. It's called forgiveness.

I'm working on it.

You triggered a strength I didn't know I had. You started me on a quest, in anger at first, to seek protection for others. I've learned much. As I've been able to help others, the place of anger has gradually eroded and has begun to fill with fresher waters of encouragement; with hope that what I've experienced and written about may open the eyes of all. I no longer hold you solely responsible. Oh yes, you were guilty of losing control, of battering a tiny bed-bound eighty-six-pound, ninety-one-year-old woman. And you've had to live with that for many years, even though you got away with it. I hope that some of the things I've learned and shared in this book will help not only the elderly and their families, but the medical people who treat them, the people who establish and oversee long-term care facilities, the people who enact laws of protection, and people like you, who must learn to cope with and control your own emotions.

We have something in common. We've "walked alone ...together" for years, neither of us knowing the other, each dealing with the fallout in our separate lives from that one incident that binds us forever. I hope you can understand that you no longer have to walk alone. You can reach out for help. I hope you already have. I hope, through cooperative efforts throughout the nation, that there will soon be a cure for this social disease called "abuse of the elderly." I've tried to do my part. Perhaps one day we'll realize that we all depend on each other, that none of us walks alone.

One person *can* make a difference!

What Can One Person Do?

One person can become an ombudsman. The State Department of Aging — Long Term Care Ombudsman Program exists in all fifty states, providing official representatives to protect the interests of residents of long-term care facilities, and to resolve problems and complaints. Under the program's authority, volunteers are trained to function in this role. This is a positive way for any individual to make a substantial, perhaps life-saving, difference. It's an especially vital service for residents without any family or personal advocate.

The effectiveness of this program will depend upon the cooperative efforts and goals of the director, the paid staff, the volunteers, and the volunteer board of directors. As a board member of the Orange County Council on Aging, I had the privilege of serving with Pamala McGovern, a leader of principle and integrity, dedicated to the interests of the residents in long-term care facilities. While the tone set by the director is important, the positive influence and efforts of a volunteer can make a significant difference, even in negative situations. If just one resident is helped, it's more than worth it.

One Person Can

"Adopt" a resident in a long-term care facility. Discover a resident who has few or no visitors. Visit. Send cards. Bring a flower. Sit and hold a hand, even if there's little response.

Learn all you can about elder issues in your area. Start a clipping file for an advocacy group or a legislator. Be sure to clip the source (newspaper or magazine name and date) for each item.

Volunteer at a local senior citizens' center, daycare center, or long-term care facility.

Write letters. To newspaper editors, to elected officials, to long-term care facility residents, or for residents unable to write their own letters. Seek out residents whose families might live in another town or state. Write for the resident, to keep the family aware of the resident's activities, general condition, and care. This point of contact could be a real service to a concerned daughter or son at a distance. And it would be great if you could encourage the family to visit an elder in one of their local facilities, to do the same thing for someone else's parent! Personal initiative in networking could improve conditions for a lot of people.

Help the activities director at a long-term care facility. Teach a craft. Play the piano for their sing-alongs. Read the newspaper aloud in the activities center. Join a clowning club that visits long-term care facilities. Enlist your teenagers, their social and service groups. Their vivacity and enthusiasm are contagious. Invite knowledgeable speakers to address your class, your church, your club, or your business on subjects of concern to elders and the sandwich generation. Be a support to advocates. Write or phone. Encourage. Listen.

One person — a member of a class, a church group, philanthropic organization, or service club — can recruit the group to become informed, to take a stand, to initiate new projects of involvement and support, to contribute financially to an advocacy organization, or take part in any of the suggestions listed above. We call these PEP Groups (People Encouraging Participation). See appendix J for suggestions.

One person in a professional capacity — physician, attorney, legislator, legislative assistant, clergy person, business person — can go the extra mile in advocacy for the elderly. Consider how you may be able to support an advocate or an advocacy group through your training, your support, your expertise, your advice, perhaps your participation on a board of directors.

What can one person do?

There is an often-quoted prayer by theologian Reinhold Niebuhr:

"O God, give us serenity to accept what cannot be changed, courage to change what should be changed, and wisdom to distinguish the one from the other."

We add, *"But God, grant us the courage not to give up on what we think is right, even though we may think it is hopeless."*

One person *can* make a difference!

Plus one, and one, and one.

And you'll never walk alone.

APPENDIX A: DEFINITIONS

Long-term Care Resident: The term "Resident" rather than "Patient" is used by designation throughout the field of eldercare as affording more dignity to the elder. The term is used in like manner throughout this book, except in discussing the doctor/patient relationship.

Nursing Home: Rather than choose a fictitious name that might coincide with a facility already in existence, we've used the generic term "nursing home" as the title of the long-term care facility where Bessie Jarvis was beaten. This is not necessarily to protect the facility, as the events that transpired there are a matter of the investigative records of several agencies. Because the problem of elder abuse is so widespread throughout the nation, the generic name suggests the need for consumers to make every effort to determine the quality of *any* facility under consideration, regardless of its reputation.

New Facility: The generic term "new facility" where Bessie Jarvis was moved after the abuse was chosen for similar reasons. There are progressive facilities that provide excellent care and make every effort to protect residents in all aspects of care. The generic term is intended to represent those kinds of facilities.

Ombudsman: Long-term Care Ombudsman Services, available in every state, found in the telephone book under government (county or state) listings, "Area Agency on Aging." An ombudsman is an impartial mediator, an advocate, mandated by state and federal law, of basic human rights of long-term care residents. Ombudsman services may vary from state to state. Check your local agency for services in your area.

The California Ombudsman services:

- Provide information to residents and their families to assist in their selection of a long-term facility—not offered by all California Ombudsman programs.

- Build a trusting relationship with the resident and help foster peace of mind.

- Investigate and help resolve complaints of neglect and abuse—mandated.

- Assist residents with resources for help with personal finances and legal problems.

- Monitor the quality of food and general healthcare—mandated.

Posey: A vest-like garment used to restrain the wearer in bed or in a chair. There are vastly differing opinions about their use. Those who favor it cite the protection factor to prevent falls. Those opposed suggest that the restraint may itself cause undue agitation and entanglement, leading to potential injury and even death. Certainly it restricts movement, leading to atrophy of bones and muscles, constipation, etc.

Case Histories: Except where permission has been granted to cite specific cases, details of cases have been modified to represent typical examples of abuse, common to an appalling number of situations nationwide.

Fictitious Names: Throughout the narrative, the names of some physicians, nurses, and long-term care residents have been changed to protect the privacy of those individuals.

APPENDIX B: WHAT IS ABUSE?

Abuse: 1. A corrupt practice or custom. 2. Improper use or treatment; misuse. 3. A deceitful act, deception. 4. Abusive language. 5. Physical maltreatment (*Webster's Seventh New Collegiate Dictionary*).

Categories of Elder Abuse

Physical Abuse: Assault and battery, slapping, beating, pinching, inflicting unnecessary pain, improper use of restraints, intentional over-use or under-use of medication, rape, sexual abuse. Watch for bruises, restraint marks, attitude changes, withdrawal, listlessness, unusual confusion, combativeness, fear, accusations, and negative reactions to facility personnel.

Mental Abuse: Threats, shouting, isolation, intimidation, ignoring. Watch for fear, withdrawal, crying, clinging, cringing, negative reactions to facility personnel, and wanting to die.

Neglect: Ignoring needs, delaying care, withholding food, water, or medical treatment, withholding assistance with personal hygiene, failure to protect from harm. Watch for skin condition — tears, redness, decubitis ulcers (bedsores) — dirty nails, unkempt hair, bad odors, dirty clothing, dirty or wet bed linen. Physical signs: weight loss, dehydration, listlessness, wandering.

Financial Abuse: Theft, misuse of funds, misuse of property. For the protection of assets, seek professional assistance.

APPENDIX C: DURABLE POWER OF ATTORNEY FOR HEALTH CARE

A durable power of attorney for health care is an important legal document that allows a trusted representative to make decisions for an elder in the event of incapacity to act on his or her own behalf. The material below is for informational purposes only. Consult with your attorney to create a legally binding document representative of your own wishes.

This document gives the person you designate as your agent the authority to make healthcare decisions for you. Your agent must act consistently with your desires as they are stated in this document or otherwise made known.

Except as you otherwise specify in it, this document gives your agent the power to consent to your doctor not giving treatment or stopping treatment necessary to keep you alive.

Notwithstanding this document, you have the right to make medical and other healthcare decisions for yourself so long as you can give informed consent with respect to the particular decision. No treatment may be given to you over your objection at the time, and healthcare necessary to keep you alive may not be stopped or withheld if you object at the time.

This document gives your agent authority to consent, refuse to consent, or withdraw consent to any care, treatment, service, or procedure to maintain, diagnose, or treat a physical or mental condition. This power is subject to any statement of your desires and any limitations you include in this document. You may state in it any types of treatment that you do not desire. A court can take away your agent's power to make healthcare decisions for you if your agent: 1. authorizes anything that is illegal; 2. acts contrary to your known desires; or 3. where your desires are not known, does anything clearly contrary to your best interests.

You have the right to revoke your agent's authority by notifying your agent or your treating doctor, hospital, or other healthcare provider orally or in writing of the revocation.

Your agent has the right to examine your medical records and to consent to their disclosure unless you limit that right in this document.

Unless you otherwise specify in it, this document gives your agent the power after you die to: 1. authorize an autopsy; 2. donate your body or parts thereof for transplant or therapeutic or educational or scientific purposes; and 3. direct the disposition of your remains.

To be valid the document must be signed and witnessed legally.

Your agent may need this document immediately in case of an emergency requiring a decision concerning your healthcare. Either keep this document where it's immediately available to your agent and alternate agents, or give each of them an executed copy. You may also want to give your doctor an executed copy.

APPENDIX D: EVALUATING AND CHOOSING A LONG-TERM CARE FACILITY

Before Placing a Loved One

Before choosing a long-term care facility, visit as many facilities as possible. Get recommendations from anyone you know who has experience with local facilities — friends, acquaintances, medical personnel, clergy. The ombudsman office is a good source for information because they visit all the facilities regularly; however, they do not make specific recommendations of facilities. (See appendix A for a detailed description of the ombudsman function.)

Keep a record of your answers to the following questions, and then compare the lists.

A. Location

Location should not be the sole factor in choosing a facility; however, successful monitoring of your loved one's care will depend to some degree upon your ability to visit often, to get there quickly in case of need, and to drop in unannounced and at varying times of day.

B. First Contact

1. *Why did you choose to visit this facility?*
   Recommended by:
   Distance from home:
   Cost factor:

2. *Did you schedule your visit by phone?*
   First contact positive?
   Are personnel friendly, well-informed?

3. *First impressions of facility:*

Clean? Does it have an odor? In caring for incontinent residents there are times when an odor is inevitable, but it should be isolated in location and duration. An overpowering scent of deodorizer is not good.

Are grounds and rooms well cared for?

Pleasant atmosphere?

4. *Facility Tour:*

Ask to see the whole facility. No area should be off-limits, except for resident privacy.

Ask to see the ombudsman poster, which, with telephone number, should be prominently displayed, in full view of public and residents.

Ask about the latest licensing inspection report. By law it must be made available to you.

Does there seem to be adequate staff? Is the staff pleasant?

How does the staff greet you? How do they treat residents?

Notice the nursing stations. Are many call buttons ringing? Is staff responding?

Sufficient staff on hand? Staff loitering around the station?

Are residents well-groomed? Notice hands and fingernails.

Are call buttons within reach? Are they plugged in?

Are water pitchers within reach? Filled with fresh water?

Are residents responsive? Contented? Lots of sleepers?

5. *Food Service:*

(*If your first visit doesn't coincide with mealtime, plan another.*)

Is the dining room pleasant? Are meals attractive?

Do residents seem to be enjoying their meals?

Ask to see trays for room-bound residents. Are they attractive?

Are room-bound residents eating? Are trays simply left on bedside tables? Is any assistance provided for those who need it? Are sluggish eaters encouraged or helped to eat? Are additional snacks available at other than mealtimes?

6. *Activities:*

Is there an activities director?

Is a schedule of activities posted?

Are residents participating?

7. *Services:*

Are barber and beautician services available by appointment?

Is a podiatrist available by appointment?

Is personal laundry service available?

Plan to drop by, unscheduled, to observe the consistency of the above factors.

8. *Make follow-up visit(s) using the same guidelines.*

APPENDIX E: PERSONAL CONSUMER RIGHTS OF THE ELDER RESIDENT

Personal consumer rights of elder residents of long-term care facilities in California are listed in Barclays California Code of Regulations (Title 22, Section 72527) and enumerated below. The ombudsman program in your state can inform you of regulations applying in your state.

(a) Patients have the rights enumerated in this section and the facility shall ensure that these rights are not violated. The facility shall establish and implement written policies and procedures which include these rights and shall make a copy of these policies available to the patient and to any representative of the patient. The policies shall be accessible to the public upon request. Patients shall have the right:

1. To be fully informed, as evidenced by the patient's written acknowledgment prior to or at the time of admission and during the stay, of these rights and of all rules and regulations governing patient conduct.

2. To be fully informed, prior to or at the time of admission and during the stay, of services available in the facility, and of related charges, including any charges for services not covered by the facility's basic per diem rate or not covered under Titles XVIII or XIX of the Social Security Act.

3. To be fully informed by a physician of his or her total health status and to be afforded the opportunity to participate on an immediate and ongoing basis in the total plan of care including the identification of medical, nursing and psychosocial needs and the planning of related services.

4. To consent to or to refuse any treatment or procedure or participation in experimental research.

5. To receive all information that is material to an individual patient's decision concerning whether to accept or refuse any proposed treatment or procedure. The disclosure of material information for administration of psychotherapeutic drugs or physical restraints or the prolonged use of a device that may lead to the inability to regain use of normal bodily function shall include the disclosure of information listed in Section 72528(b).

6. To be transferred or discharged only for medical reasons, or the patient's welfare or that of other patients or for nonpayment for his or her stay and to be given reasonable advance notice to ensure orderly transfer or discharge. Such actions shall be documented in the patient's health record.

7. To be encouraged and assisted throughout the period of stay to exercise rights as a patient and as a citizen, and to this end to voice grievances and recommend changes in policies and services to facility staff and/or outside representatives of the patient's choice, free from restraint, interference, coercion, discrimination, or reprisal.

8. To manage personal financial affairs, or to be given at least a quarterly accounting of financial transactions made on the patient's behalf should the facility accept written delegation of this responsibility subject to the provisions of Section 72529.

9. To be free from mental and physical abuse.

10. To be assured confidential treatment of financial and health records and to approve or refuse their release, except as authorized by law.

11. To be treated with consideration, respect and full recognition of dignity and individuality, including privacy in treatment and in care of personal needs.

12. Not to be required to perform services for the facility that are not included for therapeutic purposes in the patient's plan of care.

13. To associate and communicate privately with persons of the patient's choice, and to send and receive personal mail unopened.

14. To meet with others and participate in the activities of social, religious and community groups.

15. To retain and use personal clothing and possessions as space permits, unless to do so would infringe upon the health, safety or rights of the patient or other patients.

16. If married, to be assured privacy for visits by the patient's spouse and if both are patients in the facility, to be permitted to share a room.

17. To have daily visiting hours established.

18. To have visits from members of the clergy at any time at the request of the patient or the patient's representative.

19. To have visits from persons of the patient's choosing at any time if the patient is critically ill, unless medically contraindicated.

20. To be allowed privacy for visits with family, friends, clergy, social workers or for professional or business purposes.

21. To have reasonable access to telephones and to make and receive confidential calls.

22. To be free from any requirement to purchase drugs or rent or purchase medical supplies or equipment from any particular source in accordance with the provisions of Section 1320 of the Health and Safety Code.

23. To be free from psychotherapeutic drugs and physical restraints used for the purpose of patient discipline or staff convenience and to be free from psychotherapeutic drugs used as a chemical restraint as

defined in Section 72018, except in an emergency which threatens to bring immediate injury to the patient or others. If a chemical restraint is administered during an emergency, such medication shall be only that which is required to treat the emergency condition and shall be provided in ways that are least restrictive of the personal liberty of the patient and used only for a specified and limited period of time.

24. Other rights as specified in Health and Safety Code, Section 1599.1.

25. Other rights as specified in Welfare and Institutions Code, Sections 5325 and 5325.1, for persons admitted for psychiatric evaluations or treatment.

26. Other rights as specified in Welfare and Institutions Code Sections 4502, 4503 and 4505 for patients who are developmentally disabled as defined in Section 4512 of the Welfare and Institutions Code.

(b) A patient's rights, as set forth above, may only be denied or limited if such denial or limitation is otherwise authorized by law. Reasons for denial or limitation of such rights shall be documented in the patient's health record.

(c) If a patient lacks the ability to understand these rights and the nature and consequences of proposed treatment, the patient's representative shall have the rights specified in this section to the extent the right may devolve to another, unless the representative's authority is otherwise limited. The patient's incapacity shall be determined by a court in accordance with state law or by the patient's physician unless the physician's determination is disputed by the patient or patient's representative.

(d) Persons who may act as the patient's representative include a conservator, as authorized by Parts 3 and 4 of Division 4 of the Probate Code (commencing with Section 1800), a person designated as attorney in fact in the patient's valid Durable Power of Attorney for Health Care, patient's next of kin, other appropriate surrogate decision maker designated consistent with statutory and case law, a person appointed by a court authorizing treatment pursuant to Part 7 (commencing with Section 3200) of Division 4 of the Probate Code, or, if the patient is a minor, a person lawfully authorized to represent the minor.

(e) Patient's rights policies and procedures established under this section concerning consent, informed consent and refusal of treatments or procedures shall include, but not be limited to the following:

1. How the facility will verify that informed consent was obtained or a treatment or procedure was refused pertaining to the administration of psychotherapeutic drugs or physical restraints or the prolonged use of a devise that may lead to the inability of the patient to regain the use of a normal bodily function.

2. How the facility, in consultation with the patient's physician, will identify consistent with current statutory case law, who may serve as a patient's representative when an incapacitated patient has no conservator or attorney in fact under a valid Durable Power of Attorney for Health Care.

~:~

While these are the basic rights of residents in long-term care facilities as cited in California law, there is other information pertaining to rights and treatment of residents in other sections of this Title 22 document. If you have further questions we suggest you contact your local ombudsman for clarification of specific points.

Appendix F: Five-point-Plan Assessment Meeting

Sample Meeting Agenda

The initial meeting required by OBRA (Omnibus Budget Reconciliation Act of 1987, a federal regulation containing major nursing home reforms, primarily in the area of residents' rights), may not follow this specific agenda. The Five-point Plan, including the meeting agenda, was designed by the authors for the nonprofit corporation NOBLE — Network Outreach Better Living for the Elderly — to address problem solving either before or after placement. Our recommendations may be adapted to meet your specific needs.

RE: Mrs. Suzy Jones
DATE:
PLACE: Request Appropriate Office
TIME:
CALLED BY: Annie Jones, caregiver (daughter-in-law)

Introduction of Representatives to Be Present

1. Family member caregiver
2. Advocate for resident, ombudsman
3. Advocate for family
4. Administrator of facility
5. Medical professional

Concerns to Be Discussed

Examples: List any questions, special requirements, concerns (i.e., any family history that might have a bearing on resident's condition, fears, and idiosyncrasies, personal habits or desires, medical questions about treatments, things caregiver has learned at home that might benefit facility or prevent misunderstandings, etc.).

If the meeting is to resolve a specific problem after admission, list the problem, any actions previously discussed with or requested of appropriate facility personnel, verified by journal entries — see chapter 11.

Example (journal entry): "Before placing Mother here, I requested this, yet three times I have found her being bathed by a male CNA. I discussed this with the director of nursing on 4/23 and 5/2.

Specific Actions or Requests As Result of Discussion

Examples: Excessive distractive noise — radio, TV, traffic — makes resident nervous and agitated. Request a bed away from the door, or a room away from the hub of activity, etc.

Mrs. Jones is a very private person; dignity is important. Request all staff to address her as Mrs. Jones, refrain from using her first name.

Mrs. Jones is extremely modest. Please use only female aides in her personal care — bathing, toilet assistance, etc.

Mrs. Jones has indicated desire and signed authorization for "no heroic action" in the event of medical emergency. (List date of request and action agreed to; save agenda for follow-up and records.)

Closing

Thank all present for their time and attention.

Emphasize the importance of your being notified regarding any details of care, your willingness to come at any time, etc.

Note: While these are only sample suggestions, they will trigger things that are important to your particular situation. The vital thing is to express your desires/requirements and to work with the facility personnel to best carry them out.

APPENDIX G:
SAMPLE MEETING AGENDA

For Appealing Unacceptable Decision by Licensing Office

Follow the instructions given on your disposition notification regarding scheduling such a meeting.

RE: Appeal disposition in Mrs. Suzy Jones's case
DATE:
PLACE: Licensing and Certification Office (local, district, or state, depending on level of appeal)

Representatives Present

Licensing agency personnel
Family member, responsible party
Advocate for family (as in the Five-point Plan Meeting, take along an objective friend who can support your position or remind you of points to present.)
Ombudsman representative (request the presence of this advocate.)

Agenda

Be prepared to clearly state your reason for disagreeing with the findings of the investigation. Take your pictures, your care journal, any new information, and any corroborating facts.
Prepare a specific statement of what you want to see as a result of the appeal.
Ask that the case be reopened to further investigate the findings.

Closing

Thank the representatives for attending.

Ask when you might expect the findings of the new investigation.

Enter that estimate in your journal, along with any notes, questions, remarks, etc.

Appendix H: Establishing a Task Force on Elder Issues

Personnel

Sponsor: Any government official, legislator, mayor, governor, etc.

Sponsor's staff person: Deputy, assistant, aide, etc.

Person to chair: An advocate who's knowledgeable in elder issues. Could be family member advocating for abused elder. (Diane Sandell chaired a Task Force for the Elderly for her state senator.)

Ombudsman: Representative from local area Council on Aging, Ombudsman program

Other Members (as available): Professional personnel (medicine, law, legislative), disease-related organizations (Alzheimer's, Parkinson's, cancer, etc.), long-term care industry representative(s), civic personnel, service and philanthropic club members, media representatives, clergy, academia, active senior citizens, family members of elders.

Note: The sponsor and the chairperson should collectively invite, under the sponsor's auspices and signature, representatives from the fields listed above.

Schedule

Determine workable schedule (i.e., once a month for ten months, off July and August), or whatever the members decide.

Agenda

The task force Sandell chaired scheduled five meetings with guest speakers, alternating with five meetings with discussion on proposed or pending legislation, information on advocacy experience, and action and recommendations.

Guest speakers open up new aspects of advocacy. Possible speakers: ombudsman, elder-law attorneys, representative from attorney general's office, representative from senior legislature, visiting nurses, family members who've endured the trauma of dealing with the abuse of a loved one, the sponsor of the task force or assistant to address progress of legislative action, representative from long-term care industry.

Calls to the sponsor's office requesting information or help regarding elder issues would be logged. From this information, family or caregiver representatives could be invited to attend the next meeting of the task force, to relate their experiences, present their concerns, and seek help from the panel of expertise represented.

The sponsor is invited, but needn't attend every meeting; his or her administrative assistant may represent him. The purpose of the committee is to keep the legislative sponsor informed of current events, details, and recommendations.

Projects

The task force could:

~: Maintain a log (compiled by sponsor's office) of inquiries, complaints, requests regarding elder issues, to be incorporated into the discussion and action of task force.

~: Recruit volunteer news clipping services and maintain a notebook or file of news items related to elder issues.

~: Follow specific stories through to determine what conclusive action is taken.

~: Write letters to the media, requesting follow-up of related stories.

~: Publish, with the sponsor's approval and under his signature, a periodic newsletter of issues related to elder concerns, to be mailed to the sponsor's constituents.

~: Initiate recommended new or amended legislation for sponsor's consideration.

Appendix I: Starting a Caregiver Or Family Support Group

If you can't find an existing support group in your area, consider starting one. The following suggestions are offered as "thought starters" to help you plan.

Determine the Need

You yourself need help. You can be sure others are in the same situation. Ask in every situation that you find yourself in — neighbors, friends, churches, shops, etc. Write the local newspaper asking for a response from others who'd like to be in a support group.

Determine a Place and/or Sponsorship

Based on the response, decide how much room you'll need. Be creative in searching out possible locations. Churches, hospitals, schools, libraries, service clubs, banks, civic centers, and senior citizens' centers all might have rooms available for public use. If one of these groups would offer sponsorship as a civic service, it would lend credibility to the cause, but determine what they would expect or require in return. It's best not to meet in the home of one of the caregivers, so that the caregiver gets a break away from the home, but if that's the only way the group can meet, don't discard the idea.

First Meeting

1. Record names, addresses, phone numbers, and email addresses.

2. Allow a brief sharing time.

3. Ask for a list of concerns and suggested topics for discussion. Use the list to determine future agendas. Future meetings could include guest speakers on some of these topics.

4. Determine how often to meet and at what hours.

5. Establish a definite start/stop time, and adhere to it.

6. Recruit administrative help from the interests of those present — phoning, scheduling, writing notes, notifying newspaper of future meetings, etc.

7. Encourage creative suggestions; discourage "dumping." Rather than rehash negatives, people should carry away a sense of refreshment, enablement, and hope.

Appendix J: Starting a Pep (People Encouraging Participation) Club

A PEP Club can be as simple or as imaginative and creative as you want it to be.

Goal: To involve as many people as possible in making life better for the elderly.

Plan: Find a need and fill it, from the simplest to the most complex.

- It can be for any age group, from preschool classes to senior citizens' groups.

- It can be from any source of involvement: schools, churches, service clubs, neighborhood groups, employees' clubs.

- It can involve any monetary investment, from pennies to thousands of dollars.

- It can involve any time investment, from a one-time project to ongoing support.

- It can involve any activity, from entertainment or easing loneliness, to political activism (e.g., a child's group can make colorful scrapbooks; an adult group can compile and maintain information files for a task force, or write letters).

- Groups could "adopt" individual long-term care facilities, and cooperate with activities directors to provide friendship, fellowship, personal concern and caring.

- Use some of the ideas from the "One Person Can" section of chapter 17.

- Have a brainstorming party to discover new ideas.

*"... the noble man makes noble plans,
and by noble deeds he stands."*
— Isaiah 32:8, the Holy Bible

Resources

Administration on Aging
330 Independence Ave. SW # 4760
Washington, DC, 20201
202-401-4634
www.aoa.gov

American Society on Aging
833 Market St., Suite 511
San Francisco, CA, 94103
415-974-9600
www.asaging.org

Michael Leavitt, Secretary
Dept. of Health & Human Services
200 Independence Ave. SW
Washington, DC, 20201
202-619-0257
Toll Free: 877-696-6775
www.hhs.gov

National Council on Aging
1020 N. Fair Oaks Ave.
Pasadena, CA, 91103
626-791-5010
www.ncoa.org

National Family Caregivers Association
10400 Connecticut Ave., Suite 500
Kensington, MD, 20895-3944
301-942-6430
www.nfcacares.org

info@thefamilycaregiver.org

National Committee for Prevention of Elder Abuse
Institute on Aging
119 Belmont St.
Worcester, MA 01605
508-793-6166
www.preventelderabuse.org

National Association of State Units on Aging
1225 I St. NW, Room 725
Washington, DC, 20005
202-898-2578
www.nasua.org

New LifeStyles Online
www.newlifestyles.com
Lets you search for senior housing in every state

www.senior.com
Your Internet Community

www.businessandaging.com
Educational and Business Opportunities with many excellent links,
resources, and bibliography

www.healthandage.com
A positive aging newsletter

www.agenet.com
Solutions for Better Aging and Eldercare Products

www.caringcommunity.org
Pain Relief and Comfort Measures at Life's End

www.elderCoHousing.org
Possibilities for Senior Living

www.ilcusa.org
International Longevity Center; research on Aging Populations

National Organizations

www.geron.org
The Gerontological Society of America

www.asa.org
American Society on Aging

www.aghe.org
Association of Gerontological Higher Education

www.nahc.org
National Association for Home Care

www.nih.gov
National Institutes of Health

www.nia.nih.gov
National Institute on Aging/National Institutes of Health

www.aoa.dths.gov
Administration on Aging

www.creativeaging.org
Based in New York, the National Center for Creative Aging is a prime mover in shaping matters of Arts and Aging

www.Stagebridge.org
The oldest senior theater company in the US, (1978) in Oakland, CA.

www.goldenbearcasting.com/
cf: Diane Driver, Ph.D.
Resource Specialist, Resource Center on Aging
University of California, Berkeley

Recommended Reading

The 36-Hour Day: A Family Guide to Caring for People with Alzheimer Disease, Other Dementias, and Memory Loss in Later Life, 4th ed., Johns Hopkins University Press.

Add Life to Your Years, Ted W. Engstrom, Tyndale House, 2002.

A Graceful Farewell: Putting Your Affairs in Order, Maggie Watson, Cypress House, 2006.

Listening with Different Ears: Counseling People Over 60, James Warnick, QED Press, 1995.

ABOUT THE AUTHORS

A native of Kansas City, Missouri, Lois Hudson is a certified teacher, a businesswoman, and an accomplished writer. She brings a strong background in medical care to her eldercare experience, which combines fifteen years of hands-on care giving with ten years of advocacy and support through NOBLE. The mother of two grown sons, Ms. Hudson is also a proud grandmother. Currently living in Southern California, she is passionately devoted to her writing, her community, and her church.

Born in Baltimore, Maryland, homemaker and former businesswoman Diane Sandell founded NOBLE (Network Outreach—Better Living for the Elderly) to help families cope with the challenges of placing loved ones in long-term care facilities, and to help elders who have suffered institutional abuse. Her background includes twenty-five years of personal eldercare and eighteen years of advocacy on local, state, and nationwide levels. Ms. Sandell has won several community service awards for her tireless work to eradicate elder abuse.

Lois Hudson   *Diane Sandell*